DESTINY

Personal Application Guide

DESTINY

Personal Application Guide

T. D. Jakes

New York   Nashville

FaithWords

Hachette Book Group

1290 Avenue of the Americas

New York, NY 10104

www.faithwords.com

Printed in the United States of America

RRD-C

First Edition: December 2015

10 9 8 7 6 5 4 3 2 1

FaithWords is a division of Hachette Book Group, Inc.

The FaithWords name and logo are trademarks of Hachette Book Group, Inc.

The Hachette Speakers Bureau provides a wide range of authors for speaking events. To find out more, go to www.hachettespeakersbureau.com or call (866) 376-6591.

The publisher is not responsible for websites (or their content) that are not owned by the publisher.

ISBN: 978-1-4555-3465-4

Contents

CHAPTER 1

◄❖►

Understanding the Destiny Equation

"Never underestimate the power of dreams and the influence of the human spirit. We are all the same in this notion: The potential for greatness lives within each of us."

Wilma Rudolph

Are you destined for greatness? I hope that you believe you are, because that belief will be the launching pad that puts you on your personal journey toward Destiny.

What does greatness look like to you? Being destined for greatness doesn't necessarily mean acquiring fame or power or wealth. It does mean doing to the best of your ability the specific, unique task that God put you on this earth to do.

How different might your life be if you awakened every day knowing that you are engaged in what God meant for you to do? As you imagine yourself doing what only you can, know that the journey to get there will not be an ongoing rocket launch taking you higher and higher. There will be ups and downs. You will have celebrations and setbacks. Both victory and defeat will be a part of your journey.

Destiny will take you on a roller coaster of experiences that may cause you to walk in confidence one day and then shrivel in fear the next; to bask in the joy of your accomplishments one moment, and soon after wonder if it's all worth it. But it's all a part of the journey. You can't pick and choose the experiences you want and reject those you wish you didn't have to go through.

When you say yes to Destiny, you also say yes to the messy moments that are inextricably tied to the journey. Very often, the message life is teaching you lies at the center of the mess.

You cannot have progress without problems. You may look at others and think their journey was all smooth sailing, but I can guarantee that was not the case. You may never see someone else's struggle toward Destiny; but just know that it exists.

For sure, some people will look at their problems and consume themselves solely with trying to get rid of them. But when you are Destiny-driven, you can look at the problems, and even the chaos, and recognize the signs of progress within. A Destiny focus will keep you on track when it's hard to tell whether you're moving forward or falling backward.

Let's suppose you are remodeling your kitchen. Before you can get those sleek new cabinets with the granite countertops and the stainless appliances, the contractor has to tear out what's already there. As workers tear out old cabinets and rip out the old Formica countertops and perhaps even tear down a wall or two, for a few days your kitchen will look chaotic. But instead of being distressed at the sight of the demolition, you walk into the room with a smile. Why? Because you recognize the activity as a sign of progress. You understand that the old stuff has to be removed before the new features can be installed. You know your kitchen won't always look like it's been hit with a bomb. In fact, you're happy because you know that soon you'll have a better kitchen that can give you enjoyment as well as add to the value of your home.

In the personal guide, you will learn to take the messy moments as well as the mountaintop experiences and know that both are signs of progress on your journey toward Destiny. When your journey is intentional, you learn to appreciate the mess because you see advancement and evolution within the goings-on.

Destiny-mindedness teaches you to value all of your experiences. You need all the experiences, the pleasurable and the painful alike, because all of them serve to build you up so you can be ready to step into the life place that's been created just for you.

Even as you work your way through this guidebook, recognize that you are already on your Destiny journey. Take a moment to think about the major impacts on your life. Which actions or experiences had an impact on your destiny, even if you don't know what that is yet? Whether it was being raised in an extended family where everyone helped to care for your handicapped grandfather or the day you found the courage to stand up to that notorious schoolyard bully in the seventh grade, the events of your life shape you, and thereby prepare you, for Destiny.

What's Drawing You?

Mrs. Coretta King shared with me that marrying Dr. Martin Luther King Jr. and engaging in the struggle with him was her destiny. Like her, a part of me has always recognized that God was pulling me to a certain destination.

Imagine yourself, with all of your gifts and abilities, as metal. Then think of your destiny as a magnet pulling you toward its end. Where is it pulling you? Take some quiet time and consider the ways that you are drawn. What calls to you? Are the people around you always seeking your financial advice? Academic advice? Your creativity? Your organizational skills in event planning? What causes your heart to leap for joy when the magnet draws you? As you examine where you have been drawn in life, you will gain glimpses into your calling.

List the areas where you are consistently drawn. If you cannot list specific areas, then give general categories.

_____ _____

_____ _____

_____ _____

Has your destiny been confirmed for you, or are you still searching for the way? What life signs confirm for you that you have a purpose to fulfill that no one else can do?

_____ _____

_____ _____

_____ _____

Think about what is drawing you. God is not pulling your contaminants, but the pure self that resides at your core. During the 1800s, gold miners in California were looking for the gold, not the dirt and rocks and unusable parts. But they had to sift through it all to get to what was valuable. God is looking for that which has value. So think of your life experiences as a sifting process that is separating you from fears, insecurities, superficialities, anxieties, and the like.

Paint Your Canvas

Have you identified the gifts that come naturally to you? Perhaps you have a flair for remodeling old furniture and making it into something innovative. Think about what you put your mind or your hands to that transforms you into a Pablo Picasso with your unique canvas. Just like LeBron James with a basketball, or world-renown neurosurgeon Dr. Ben Carson with a scalpel, or Aretha Franklin with a microphone, you have a personal canvas given to you by Destiny to make a personal impression on this life.

After you've devoted some time to consider your special form of artistry, use a blank sheet of paper as the canvas to draw a picture of you in your destiny. If you're drawing abilities are really, really, bad, use images cut from magazines and paste them to your blank canvas. Seeing your canvas come to life should excite you, because it's you doing what you truly love.

You Can't Fool Destiny

Years ago, a popular television commercial featured a woman as Mother Nature. She became angry and invoked her wrath because she was fooled into thinking that a brand of margarine was actually butter. Destiny can't be fooled like that. Either you will operate authentically or you will never get to the place where you belong.

Your engagement in pursuits that are your authentic calling may be a natural outgrowth of the circuitous path of Destiny, or you may simply be emulating the behavior of another whose path appeals to you. You many dabble in many endeavors before you stumble upon the right life space, but Destiny will not cooperate in drawing you where you do not belong.

Are you currently engaged in pursuits that do not genuinely reflect your destined purpose? If you are, then devise a plan to wean them from your life. If you are involved in volunteer work that, though worthwhile, may only be distracting you from Destiny, it's time to plan for some changes.

Develop a plan that will allow you to leave the well-paying, dead-on job that depletes your time and energy for living your true life. Establish a general time line and a plan for making transitions, especially those that can impact other people, like your spouse, your children, your parents, and so forth. Your plan may be open for revision as you complete the book, so do your writing in pencil or on computer!

So . . . You're Not There Yet

Destiny may seem a trillion miles away. Unreachable, unattainable, impossible . . . these may be words you have uttered as you consider your life's dream. Don't give up because Destiny comes in steps. The elevation to your highest calling is not an elevator ride that smoothly and seamlessly transports you from one level to the next. Nor is your journey an escalator ride that takes you higher and higher once you step on.

The elevator is unreliable and the escalator can only take you so far. Arriving at the place to which you were called means taking the stairs. Step by step you will move into the place that has been divinely planned for you. Going up with every step, you'll get tired. The next landing will seem like an eternity away. Just keep walking. Repeat a mantra from *The Little Engine that Could*, if you have to. The important thing is that you keep on walking.

God has kept you through things . . . sickness, sin, problems, enemies, weaknesses, insecurities, disappointments, and even wrongdoings. Why would God have kept you, even when you were wrong, if what is planned for you wasn't greater than what is behind you? The only reason you have been pulled back into what is behind you is because you keep looking back. God's not the one who's taking you there.

Who Inspires You?

Write down the name of one person who inspires you to remain faithful to the steps Destiny requires. Think about why that person's journey motivates you to keep going. Create a list of characteristics the person displays and think about how those same traits can help you on your journey to Destiny.

Them   *Me*

_____   _____

_____   _____

_____   _____

_____   _____

Looking Through the Lens of Destiny

Destiny's call to greatness also means a call to accept the challenges of life. Mrs. Coretta King understood her calling to be married to the world's most famous civil rights leader. In the Bible, Moses was a man whose destiny necessitated a series of changes and trials. Think about the challenges you've faced. Take a new look at the obstacles you've overcome through the lens of Destiny. Reflect on the growth that came from those experiences, even though you may have despised your circumstances at the time.

_____

_____

_____

_____

_____

You Are More Than What You Have

Place two clear glasses or jars on a table. Now open a bag of dry beans or marbles. Place a piece of tape on the side of each jar. On the jar on the right, write MY POSSESSIONS.

On the jar on the left, write ME. Think about who you are and what you have. For every possession or relationship associated with you, put a bean/marble in the jar on the right. For every adjective that describes you or your abilities, put a bean/marble in the left jar. Think of as many things as you can as quickly as you can. When you complete the exercise, there should be more beans/marbles in the jar that describes you than in the jar that describes your possessions.

If you have more objects in your possessions jar, reflect on whether you have been defining yourself according to your possessions rather than on who you are and how you have been gifted to perform your unique earth assignment. Then spend some time in prayer or meditation over how your life can be aligned so that you are more Destiny focused than possession-oriented.

> Destiny is the culmination of connecting the push of our instincts to the pull of our purpose.
>
> *Bishop T. D. Jakes*

What Are Your Destiny Steps?

Write your name in the center of the circle. Then, think about some of your experiences that have shaped you into who you are. Think about the unique journey that is your life and consider how each has molded, shaped and sculpted you into who you have become and who you will be in the future. College, marriage, illness, childbirth, bankruptcy, death, promotion, new house all can be just some of the life events that are shaping you into a person of Destiny.

As you consider these events, also think about how you should begin to look at your life experiences in the future.

Moments of Perfect Timing

Consider the serendipitous moments of your life that equated to perfect timing. Think about whether such instances confirm that the events of your life are orchestrated and strategized by a power greater than yourself.

Also think about the things in your life that might have happened, but did not, and the disastrous results you avoided because of it. Consider whether these moments also affirm your predestined assignment.

Take a Destiny Step

Write down a single, reasonable, and realistic action you will take toward Destiny upon completing chapter one.

_____

_____

_____

_____

_____

CHAPTER 2

❖

Wanting More Is Not a Lack of Gratitude

"God has created you with the raw materials you need to reach your destiny."
Bishop T. D. Jakes

We live in a culture that encourages us to want more. Nearly every commercial we see on television will lead us to believe that purchasing the advertised product or service will bring fulfillment. From automobiles to weekend getaways, we're encouraged to want more; and further, to think that happiness depends on greater procurement.

The mere acquisition of more does not bring happiness or fulfillment, however. So when the magnet of Destiny is drawing the metal that is the essence of who we are, we may tend to dismiss that as well. That's when it's time to pay attention. The more that feeds your spirit is the lure of Destiny.

It's always a good idea to improve yourself and attain more. But it is important to know why you want it. Do you want more because you think a higher status will improve your self-esteem? Do you want more so you can feel like you're as good as or better than other people?

The more you seek should always be rooted in a desire to serve humanity in greater ways rather than making you superior. The more that is the mere acquisition of things is not a step toward Destiny. Rather, it is a step toward unfulfillment and misery because you're looking for something outside of you to validate your existence.

Use the circle below to write in it the things in your life that you truly feel good about. For example, job promotion, spouse, family, advanced degree, new home or car, good health, weight loss, and so forth. Fill in the circle as much as you can. Now, outside the circle, write the more that you long for in your life. The things you write may be physical, material or spiritual, but as you write them, be sure to know how the acquisition of it can help you on the road to your destiny.

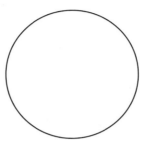

Now, compare what is inside your circle with what is outside your circle. Does wanting the things outside your circle make you feel greedy or ungrateful for what you have? Or, can you see how acquiring the things outside your circle help you to become a better person and fulfill your destiny?

Destiny Is Calling

The yearning for more inside you calls to you just like the instinctive call that goes out to a baby chick, telling her to start pecking out of the shell that confines her.

How can you begin the process of pecking your way out of the space that has become too small for you?

First, recognize that the space has become too small, then write some ideas about how you may begin extricating yourself from that confinement and grow into a larger arena. For example, your home may be too small for your growing family. Your job may feel more like a prison cell than a stepping-stone to Destiny. Think about what causes you to feel held back, and then consider how you can take a step to change.

Area of My Life   *First Step to Change*

_____   _____

_____   _____

_____   _____

_____   _____

There Is Always More You Can Do!

Have you stamped *ne plus ultra* on some area of your life? Have you told yourself that you're too old to start a new career, go back to school or fall in love? Do you think that you can never reach a goal you've always longed to achieve? Dare to dream! Write down your *ne plus ultras* and think about how your thinking or your situation can be changed so that there is more beyond the door you thought was closed.

_____   _____

_____   _____

_____   _____

_____   _____

"The only thing we have to fear is fear itself."

Franklin Delano Roosevelt

Fear Clouds the Issue

Fear keeps people from doing many of the things they want. Sometimes the fear is their own. Sometimes the fear is fueled by the concerns of the people who love them. President Roosevelt showed great wisdom with his cautionary words to a nation facing the worst economic disaster in its history. There were real issues to be afraid of during the Great Depression—hunger, homelessness, disease, and unemployment. As commander-in-chief, he was not downplaying the significance of these difficulties. Rather, he cautioned against being consumed with panic that fuels an irrational mind-set, which leads to unreasonable and illogical behavior that would only worsen their predicament.

What are you afraid of to the extent that it hinders your ability to do the things you want? Fill a clean, clear jar with water, leaving about two inches clear at the top. Place the jar on a table next to a small mound of dirt. Imagine that the jar of water represents the place you want to be—fresh, uncluttered and clear. Now think about the fears you have associated with getting closer to your destiny, whether they are your own or those of a loved one. For example, your spouse or parent may have expressed concerns about you quitting your job to pursue a vocation you've always dreamed of. As you think of those fears, drop a teaspoon of dirt into the jar of water. Keep putting in small amounts of dirt, representing all of your fears.

When you're done, look carefully at your jar of water. Is the water still clear enough to see through? Is the water so cloudy and dirty that you can't see through it? Make a connection between being unable to see your way and staying in small spaces. When your vision is unclouded, you will be more willing to venture into a larger arena. As you look at the jar of dirty water, think about how you can clear the air of fear in your own life and see your way clear to fulfill your dreams.

_____

_____

_____

_____

Livin' Small

Livin' large is an urban phrase indicating a life that is full and prosperous. It's the good life that people aspire to and rejoice in while others brag on it. Nobody brags about someone who's living small, yet so many people do because they're afraid to stretch, afraid to hope, or afraid of failure.

It's easy to point out the shortcomings of someone else who has failed to live up to the fullness of his or her potential. Think about someone you know like that. Write down a few ways that you know the person is living a life that is too small. Place a check mark by the actions or characteristics that could also be true of your own life.

_____

_____

_____

_____

Illuminate Your Soul

People who can inspire you are all around; just like those you know who have failed to live up to their potential. Think about a person or an instance that really inspired you to know that you should not give up, just like my dad waiting all day at the furniture store for those lamps let me know that I should not let go of what I desire.

Think about that story again and again. What are the elements of the story that confirm tenacity is worth the energy required to go after what you desire? Think about the feelings you had as you recalled the story and hold on to them as you think about reaching your own destiny.

Write a few lines about someone who inspires you toward your destiny and why.

_____

_____

_____

_____

_____

_____

You're Still Standing!

If you like a good movie where the protagonist defeats the enemy after a great struggle, take some time to watch your favorite. We all cheer for the person who takes a hit and gets back up again, much like the mythical fighter Rocky Balboa, portrayed in the movies bearing his name. He was a boxer who took many hard hits, yet he kept getting back up.

The ability to stand is much like the inflatable punching plaything many of us had as children. You know the one where you punch it and it keeps popping back upright every time. Consider treating yourself to one of these toys to encourage your adult emotions. Each time you punch it, think about all the times you've been knocked down and kept getting back up. And, just like the resolute toy, you will continue to stand!

Write down the three biggest battles of your life. Next to each one, write "I'm still standing!" Use the fact that you've survived as fuel to encourage you to keep going, knowing that other obstacles will come, but that you will overcome them also.

Write "I'm still standing" on the three short lines below, representing the unknown challenges you will face. Know and have the confidence that whatever comes your way, you will overcome and continue to stand!

_____   _____

_____   _____

_____   _____

Know the Difference

What do you think is the difference between a fight and a hindrance? Think about the challenges you currently face. Which ones will require you to fight and which are merely hindrances that require only a bit of energy?

Knowing the difference will keep you from expending energy on matters that don't merit it. Understanding what deserves a fight will help you train for and focus on what doing battle over really matters.

Fight!	*Let it go!*
_____	_____
_____	_____
_____	_____

There Are Setbacks and There Are Setups

Sometimes the worst thing that happened to you is the best thing that could have happened to you. That's when you can look back over your trouble and be glad. Financial, romantic, professional or physical setbacks can often morph into a setup for something extraordinary to occur.

When have your setbacks become setups for a greater opportunity? Think about such a time in your or in someone else's life and extract some lessons from it that can help you the next time you face a setback.

_____

_____

_____

_____

_____

My, How You've Grown!

How tall were you when you started your journey to Destiny? How tall have you grown as a result of your challenges, obstacles and victories? Do you still have room to grow? You likely have experienced incremental growth spurts in various areas of your life. For a time you may grow intellectually, and then you may grow spiritually, then professionally.

Create your own growth chart and determine where you are on your journey. Use the silhouettes on the following chart to mark your levels of growth educationally, professionally, emotionally and spiritually. Compare your level of growth in each of these levels and determine how you can have more balanced, well-rounded growth in preparation for your destiny.

Do you remember when you were a kid and your grandmother or uncle saw and remarked, "My, how you've grown!"? You have no trouble gauging how you've grown physically, but you may be challenged to assess your growth in other areas.

In order to get a more balanced view of how you've grown in various areas and completing the following chart, consider talking to someone who's known you for a while—perhaps a relative or a friend who will tell you the truth. Ask them to share their insights into how you've grown in a certain area.

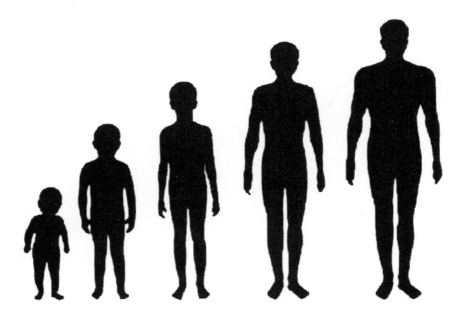

Can you identify the current experiences in your life that may help you develop and grow in personal ways? For example, have you had encounters that are helping you grow in maturity, compassion, empathy, etc.? Why are traits such as these important to your destiny?

_____

_____

_____

_____

_____

A mustard seed is a tiny speck that measures only about one or two millimeters in diameter. Yet the small seed can produce a plant that can grow as tall as nine feet. What God has seeded in you may seem very small, but you have the potential to use what is there and grow tall into your destiny.

Make a list of the raw materials you believe God has given you that will help you in your pursuit of Destiny.

_____   _____

_____   _____

_____   _____

_____   _____

_____   _____

_____   _____

Greatness Inspires Greatness

Who are the people and what are the environments that inspire you to be greater? Who are the people you need to spend more time with to inspire you to be your best self? Who can teach you more about your profession?

Devise a strategy for legitimately spending more time around such people (i.e., volunteer work, joining a profession organization, social media connection, etc.).

What are the environments that inspire you to be greater and how can you spend more time in such spaces?

_____

_____

_____

_____

_____

You Are an Original

Great people will inspire you and motivate you, but you are unique. Create a product label about yourself, using single-word descriptions that highlight your unique qualities. For example, you may write Tenacious, Genius, Talented, Smart, Sophisticated, Educated, Mature, Intelligent, and so forth. Put your picture on the label and make it an advertisement of you. In other words, imagine you are selling a package of you.

There's Always Something to Gain

In the movie *With Honors*, actor Joe Pesci picked up a stone to remind him of his major life experiences. Every occurrence in your life will not be one of great heights, but they all play a role in your destiny. You will gain something from every encounter.

Think about your current involvements and experiences. What can you take away from them? What will be your takeaway from the job that is not your dream occupation? What will you gain from the relationship that has no marriage potential? What will you learn from the class that has nothing to do with your major?

When we look for our experiences to be beneficial, we are much more likely to learn from them and gain insights that can be helpful in the future.

Take a walk and find a few small stones. Use a marker to write one of your major life areas on each stone, especially the areas that you are hoping for improvement. For example, the name of the company where you work, the department you work in, the neighborhood where you live, an adversary in the community or even your marriage. As you look at each stone, think about how the experience is improving you and preparing you for Destiny, even though you may be frustrated by it. Keep the stones in a special container and look at them occasionally to remember that every challenge also yields a benefit. None of your time or your experiences is wasted.

Where Did That Come From?

During the years of the popular Oprah Winfrey show, occasionally the queen of talk featured an episode called "Wildest Dreams" where she fulfilled the most amazing imaginings of a few people—visions of a new house, an encounter with a favorite performer, or a guest role on a television series.

Imagine you are a guest contestant on a show called *Your Wildest Dreams* and God is the host. What would be your wildest Destiny dream? What would you ask for that you've seen in your imagination, but thought would never come true?

You will be more focused toward Destiny if you have a clear vision of where you are headed.

_____

_____

_____

_____

_____

Balance Is Key

Life often feels like a juggling act for people who are highly goal oriented. But when your life is out of balance, it's difficult to maintain focus. Getting things done and taking care of your duties means balancing your time among all of your responsibilities. That doesn't mean every commitment will gain equal share every day but understanding the extent of your obligations and the time they demand will help you with time management.

Think about the major responsibilities you are juggling. Use each of the plates to name a specific duty and estimate how much time it requires on an average day. Look at all of your commitments and determine whether some realignment is needed in one or more areas. Some areas may need more time, others less. Some areas can likely be eliminated from your cycle of concern.

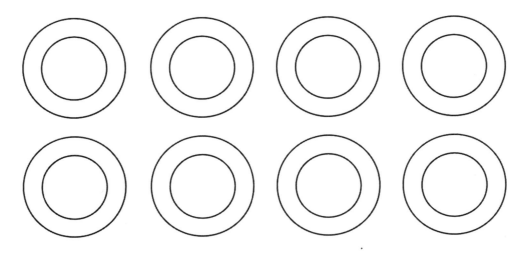

Take a Destiny Step

Think about the areas of your life that need more focus and the areas that you need to let go of. Write down what you intend to do to help you give greater focus to your destiny.

_____

_____

_____

_____

_____

CHAPTER 3

✦

Respect the Steps

"Successful people maintain a positive focus in life no matter what is going on around them. They stay focused on their past successes rather than their past failures, and on the next action steps they need to take to get them closer to the fulfillment of their goals rather than all the other distractions that life presents to them."

Jack Canfield

Every so often you may feel extra good or energetic and decide to take on a flight of stairs with gusto. You may tackle them two by two, and it feels great. But that's an occasional thing. You can't take every flight of steps by skipping as many steps as you can. Sometimes they just have to be taken a single rung at a time.

The journey toward Destiny is the same way. Occasionally, you can skip a step here or there, but Destiny's trek is a one-at-a-time undertaking. At times your Destiny climb may seem like walking the stair-climber at the gym. You keep climbing and climbing, step after step, but it seems like you're getting nowhere. It may seem that way for weeks, until you look in the mirror or step on the scale and see that all of your hard work is paying off.

Your Destiny trek can seem to be going nowhere, until one day you take an honest assessment of your past and your present and realize that you've made genuine progress.

Look at the following staircase and write down the most important steps you have taken toward Destiny. The more important the step, the higher you should position the step on the ladder.

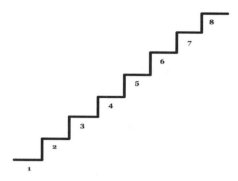

Look at what you have written on the steps and think about how each has created readiness in you for what lies ahead. Now, reflect on the blessings you have been given that you may not have been ready to handle—a job, a large sum of money, a relationship, an automobile, and so forth. How would you handle the situation differently today?

What I Got	*What I Did*	*What I Would Do Differently*

Establishing an agenda keeps you focused. That is true for meetings and it's true for life in general. It's also true for your day-to-day living. Part of your daily schedule may include going to work or school, feeding your children and getting them off to school, and getting an oil change for your car.

Think about everything you did on the last business day of this week. If you're completing this on a Saturday, what did your Friday agenda look like? Write down what you did in a 24-hour period to help you gain insight into how you are spending your time. After reviewing your daily agenda, contemplate how your life is ordered and give consideration as to whether you are truly focused on Destiny.

Then complete a second schedule that reflects what you would like for your daily agenda to look like. Are you negotiating contracts for a major corporation? Would your activities include taking college or specialty courses? Are you running a homeless shelter for families? Are you working out and preparing meals that are healthy and nutritious? Are you spending more time with family and less at work?

As you look over your completed actual schedule, consider what it reveals about your priorities and whether you have an agenda that supports a Destiny-centered lifestyle. If not, think about some changes you need to make. Are you spending too much time sleeping, socializing or working? Where does your life need balance?

Compare your actual daily agenda with your desired schedule. How does the life you have differ from the life you want? What steps can you take right now to make the life you have the life you want? Where can you make changes in your life that prioritize fulfilling your dream?

My Daily Agenda

6a		6p	
7a		7p	
8a		8p	
9a		9p	
10a		10p	
11a		11p	
12p		12a	
1p		1a	
2p		2a	
3p		3a	
4p		4a	
5p		5a	

My Desired Agenda

6a		6p	
7a		7p	
8a		8p	
9a		9p	
10a		10p	
11a		11p	
12p		12a	
1p		1a	
2p		2a	
3p		3a	
4p		4a	
5p		5a	

Who Are You to Dream?

It takes daring to dream! You need bravery to believe that you can grow from your present circumstances to a higher plane. An acorn has the audacity to grow from a small nut to a huge tree because the acorn has everything inside that is necessary to become a mighty oak.

You can dare to dream because God has already placed greatness inside of you! From the day you were conceived, God imbued you with gifts and abilities that are to be used to accomplish great, even miraculous things. Some people know those gifts within themselves from a very young age. For others, their special talents evolve over time.

Use these acorns to identify what got planted in you from birth in order that you can fulfill your destiny. Connect them to the great and powerful person you will become, like the mighty oak that stands strong and tall!

Are You Ready?

Find an opportunity to observe someone who is already doing what you desire to do in fulfillment of your destiny. Whether you want to enter medicine, run a non-profit

organization, raise children or be a college professor, you will definitely benefit from having firsthand knowledge of the sacrifices needed to achieve what you desire.

If you can't shadow someone in person, perhaps you can look at interviews or activities of such persons online. Talk to the person. Ask questions. Discover the potential cost of your success. Are you willing to make the investment to gain knowledge, internships, training, study, financial sacrifice, time from family and socializing?

If you're not ready, get in a quiet place and meditate on these three questions: (1) Am I willing to make the sacrifices needed to get ready? (2) Am I ready to get ready? (3) Can my desire to get ready be sustained?

Prioritize, Focus, Ignore

God created in you a gifted human being, but even with all your talent, you are a limited resource. There's only so much you can accomplish in any given day; therefore, three important abilities to becoming Destiny-ready are the capacity to prioritize, focus and ignore. If you don't do all three, you may spend time majoring on minor issues while completely ignoring important tasks.

You'll probably be better at one more than the other two. You may be able to focus well, but not prioritize. You may be able to ignore, but not focus as well as you should.

List the areas in your life where you need to do each. There may be some things you are focused on, but you need to prioritize them. You may have ignored some duties you need to prioritize. You may be focused on something you need to ignore. As you write down the areas that you prioritize, focus and ignore, circle the tasks that need to go to another column.

Prioritize	*Focus*	*Ignore*
_____	_____	_____
_____	_____	_____
_____	_____	_____
_____	_____	_____
_____	_____	_____

Establish your personal priorities so that you live your authentic life. What are the things you want to prioritize, versus what you actually do prioritize?

_____

_____

_____

_____

Own It!

Ownership is a great accomplishment, but it also requires great responsibility. Owning your first home is an exhilarating feeling. But the maintenance and repairs may leave you feeling drained at times. Having your own business is a great achievement, but the onus lies with you as the proprietor. Whether it's a car, a business, or a model's walk on the runway, owning the place where you are as well as the place you are trying to go means making a commitment to it.

You can't have commitment phobia if you ever intend to own something. I know people who lived their entire lives without ever owning anything—not a house, a car, a relationship or a child. Not that a person can be owned; but rather, they live without ever making the commitment to stick with something, like we must do when we take ownership.

How do you own your destiny? Can you handle the glory and the garbage that goes with it? How will owning it affect how you think? How you dress, walk or talk? How you interact with others? How you take care of yourself? Will the people with whom you choose to associate change as you own it?

_____

_____

_____

_____

What are some ways you have been sidetracked from Destiny, whether or not the activity you engaged in was a good, helpful deed or not? Was it the right thing to do? Would you have felt guilty by saying "No" to each of those tasks?

_____

_____

_____

_____

_____

_____

_____

Do you try to explain or rationalize your devotion to your destiny? You really don't have to explain your actions to anyone, but take the time here to craft a positive response to any negative impressions about why you are devoted to making your dream happen.

_____

_____

_____

_____

_____

_____

_____

There is a difference between living and existing. It's one thing to have a full life in which you engage every day, where you are fully present. It's quite another to simply exist, to have a perfunctory lifestyle where you gain nothing and give nothing.

Complete the following sentences. Decide whether to insert the word *living* or *existing*.

A person who is _____ talks to his boss about how to make improvements in the workplace, while the person who is _____ puts up with everything that goes on simply to get his paycheck.

A person who is _____ prayerfully considers the right time to talk with her husband about an important matter affecting their household, while the person who is _____ quietly hopes the issue will go away. A person who is _____ waits for life to present opportunities, while a person who is _____ actively pursues them.

What, for you, means the difference between being alive and living on life support? Where do you feel that you fall currently on the scale below? Rate yourself, keeping in mind that people on life support are dependent on external stimuli to keep them alive.

1	2	3	4	5	6	7	8	9	10
Life Support									Authentic Living

People engaged in authentic living thrive on impacting their world based on what is inside of that is eager to come out. Reflect on how much of your quality of life depends on people and circumstances, rather than the motivation of an inner vision.

Have you ever fought divine order? Think about some of the life circumstances you have resisted, either because you didn't plan it or because it produced discomfort. Hopefully, over time, the situation made sense to you and you understood the benefit that came from it.

What are some of the divinely ordered circumstances you've faced and how did they evolve into something beneficial?

_____

_____

_____

_____

_____

_____

_____

_____

What needs to be cut loose from your life so that it will not interfere with Destiny? What stops you from extricating yourself?

What I need to let go...   *What stops me...*

_____   _____

_____   _____

_____   _____

_____   _____

As you fill in the blanks, consider whether the things you are holding on to are worth the price of hindering Destiny.

Take a Destiny Step

Take a sheet of paper and write down the major things that hinder you from your destiny. Then use a pair of scissors to cut away the thing you are willing to separate yourself from. What are you willing to cut yourself away from in order to clear your course to Destiny?

_____

_____

_____

_____

CHAPTER 4

✦

Sifting Through What Matters Most

"I know that each of us has much to do. Sometimes we feel overwhelmed by the tasks we face. But if we keep our priorities in order, we can accomplish all that we should. We can endure to the end regardless of temptations, problems, and challenges."

Joseph B. Wirthlin

There's a story about where people belong in the theater of your life. Some can be trusted with a front-row seat while others must be relegated to the balcony, if you are to relate to them at all. It's been asserted that some people can only get to the parking lot, while still others can only drive around the block!

"Everyone Can't Be in Your FRONT ROW"

Life is a theater so invite your audiences carefully. Not everyone is holy enough and healthy enough to have a FRONT ROW seat in our lives.

There are some people in your life that need to be loved from a distance.

It's amazing what you can accomplish when you let go of at least minimize your time with draining, negative, incompatible, not-going-anywhere relationships, friendships, fellowships and family!

Everyone can't be in Your FRONT ROW.

Observe the relationships around you. Pay attention to: Which ones lift and which ones lean?

Which ones encourage and which ones discourage?

Which ones are on a path of growth uphill and which ones are just going downhill?

Everyone can't be in Your FRONT ROW.

When you leave certain people, do you feel better or feel worse?

Which ones always have drama or don't really understand, know and appreciate you and the gift that lies within you?

Everyone can't be in Your FRONT ROW.

The more you seek God and the things of God, the more you seek quality, the more you seek not just the hand of God but the face of God, the more you seek things honorable, the more you seek growth, peace of mind, love and truth around you, the easier it will become for you to decide who gets to sit in the FRONT ROW and who should be moved to the balcony of your life.

Everyone can't be in Your FRONT ROW.

You cannot change the people around you... but you can change the people you are around!

Ask God for wisdom and discernment and choose wisely the people who sit in the FRONT ROW of your life.

Remember that FRONT ROW seats are for special and deserving people and those who sit in your FRONT ROW should be chosen carefully.

Everyone can't be in Your FRONT ROW.

Since you can't change the people in your life, perhaps you should change the people in your life! In other words, you can't change another person, but you can change who you choose to associate with.

Do you have people who are more draining than invigorating? Maybe it's time to adjust some relationships. Use the following theater chart to position the relationships in your life. You are on the stage of your life.

Write the names of people who are on the front row, the balcony and every place in between. Are there people who need to change their seating? There may even be some who need to be in the parking lot rather than inside! Maybe you've been keeping someone on the periphery of you life who needs to move closer. Circle the names of people who need to move and draw an arrow to the place they need to occupy.

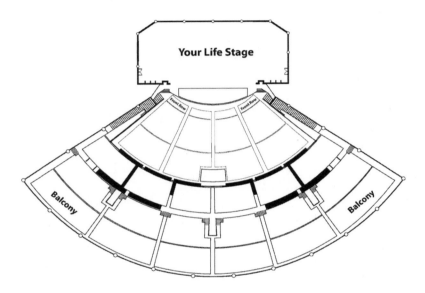

Know Who You Are

It's important to know who you are apart from what you have. God wants to use the real you, not the executive, not the husband, not the mother, not the politician, not the millionaire.

Write down twelve words that describe you that have nothing to do with what you have, a role you play, or a position you occupy. What you are writing should describe the traits you have that God can use for Destiny.

_____ _____ _____

_____   _____   _____

_____   _____   _____

_____   _____   _____

Who's Who?

You already have people in your life who are Constituents, Comrades, and Confidantes. Think about twenty-four people in your life who impact your destiny. Use the three columns to designate how those twenty-four fit into your life.

Think about the people you trust most, the people who are with you whether you are riding high or slumping low. Those are Confidantes. You may have a few more Comrades that you work with or collaborate with on various projects or issues. You may have quite a few Constituents who may be with you today and not tomorrow. You probably will not have an equal distribution in the three columns. You likely will have few Comrades, and even fewer Confidantes.

Constituents	*Comrades*	*Confidantes*

Can You Afford Your Destiny?

Finances are an important component of Destiny, especially if your economic condition is a hindrance to you achieving your dreams. Financial freedom makes the difference if you want to quit your job and go back to school or start your own business.

Write down your expenses for one month. Look at where your money is spent to determine if you are literally putting your money where your mouth is!

Align where your money is spent with your ability to pursue your life's calling. Looking at your spending will tell you whether you're investing too much of your budget on restaurants or leisure travel, on the car you bought or on clothes. A look at your assets will tell you a lot about what you prioritize. You're not crafting a budget here, just taking a general look at where your resources go.

Monthly Income	$
Current Housing Expenses	**Average Monthly Expenses**
Rent/ Mortgage	$
Utilities (If paid separately)	$
Current Non-Housing Expenses	**Average Monthly Expenses**
Food	$
Clothing	$
Day Care/Tuition	$
Car Loan	$
Car Insurance	$
Gas and Oil	$
Car Repairs	$
Other Transportation	$
Debt Payments	$
Entertainment	$
Taxes	$
Insurance	$
Telephone	$
Other (specify)	$
Total Monthly Expenses	$

What Gets Your Attention?

When issues come across your mental radar, you have a choice whether to deal with it or let it pass because it isn't worth your time. Read the following scenarios and consider whether you would deem them worthy of your attention.

☐ A trusted co-worker comes to your office and tells you that an office worker has suggested that you got your recent promotion because you're having an affair with the owner of the company. You know that you got the new position because you've earned it and you're qualified to do the job.

☐ Your son comes home and tells you he got into an argument on the basketball court. The other player yelled a derogatory remark at him. Their coach talked to both of them and the player gave your child a half-hearted apology.

☐ A group of people you associate with regularly pride themselves on the expensive clothes they wear and the luxury cars they drive. One of them occasionally teases you because you drive a regular car and wear quality, but not overly expensive clothes. Several people in the group have been helpful to you as you build your business, so you want to maintain the associations.

Sometimes it's difficult to choose what deserves your attention and what you can afford to ignore, especially when emotions are involved. Being Destiny-focused can help train your mind to determine what will move off your mental radar on its own.

Can I Get a Lift?

Destiny will bring all kinds of people to you along the way. Pay attention to who you choose to stay around. Persons who are smarter than you have the capacity to help you broaden your knowledge and exposure, just as you can help others who have not learned as much as you.

Think about your friends and associates. How many are smarter or further along than you and can help you become better? How many are not as smart as you and cause you to feel smarter? If you're the smartest one in every area of your life, it's time to think about why that is so.

Be honest as you list names below:

Who am I smarter than?   *Who's smarter than me?*

_____   _____

_____   _____

_____   _____

_____   _____

_____   _____

Going With the Flow

God has already designed your purpose. It's up to you to follow the path, with all of its ebbs and flows. Sometimes you may resist where God is leading you because the place is unfamiliar, or even downright uncomfortable.

When you're challenged by circumstances, it becomes hard to let go and let God and feel reassured that as out of control as it may feel to you, your situation is not out of divine control.

Find an online sound file or video that gives the sound of moving water, whether a babbling brook, a river or an ocean (or use a sound machine, if you have one). Listen to the sound as you consider a situation in your life that feels out of your control. Close your eyes and listen to the sound of the moving water. Imagine yourself going in the same direction as the water, not resisting or fighting. See yourself going with the flow of your circumstances and relax in the knowledge that God is the mastermind that orchestrates it all.

Going with the flow can be especially important when we have the experience of being emptied of something. Human beings don't like the feeling of emptiness, so we tend to fill voids as they occur, rather than waiting for God to fill them according to the divine plan for our life direction.

What are your favorite or regular means of filling voids? People use all sorts of things—like shopping, drugs, food, relationships, busyness, and religion—to eliminate the feeling of emptiness. While all of these things serve a beneficial purpose when used properly, they become a detriment when they simply satisfy our longing to be rid of hollowness.

Take some time to think about the limitations of using things or people to fill voids rather than trusting God to complete us and relieve us of feelings of emptiness.

Take a Destiny Step

What are some things you have prioritized over following God's plan for your life? What can you do to convince yourself that Destiny is more important than the distractions you've allowed?

_____

_____

_____

_____

_____

CHAPTER 5

▰◈▰

Who Are You, Really?

"Look at the evidence and to be willing to question your own truths, and to be willing to scrutinize things that you hold dearly because that way, that transparency, that self-awareness, will protect you from ever becoming somebody that whose beliefs somehow make them have myopic vision about what could be."

Jason Silva

The Bible says that your gifts will make room for you. How has the world opened doors and made room for you to use the abilities God has given you?

_____

_____

_____

_____

_____

_____

Ask someone you know, such as a co-worker or casual friend to share how they and other people perceive you. Write their comments in the column on the left. On the right, put down your authentic attributes.

Look at both lists. Circle the traits that represent the public you on the right. Then circle the descriptives that depict the private you on the left. As you look at the two lists, think about the importance of maintaining a private you and a public you and how that differs from being disingenuous.

Why is it important to maintain your private self and what might be the consequences of failing to do so?

Public Me   *Private me*

_____   _____

_____   _____

_____   _____

_____   _____

I need to respect my need to maintain a private self because:

_____

_____

_____

You Gotta Pay the Bills

What are the bills you have paid thus far on your Destiny journey? What seeds have you sown into Destiny so that you can reap a harvest? What apprenticeships or volunteer programs have you entered just to get the training? What lower paying jobs have you taken in order to get an understanding of the industry where you want to work? What clients have you helped for free just so you could gain the experience?

Look at the activities and experiences you've had and determine how you believe they are part of you paying the price of Destiny.

Truthfully, you will never know how the seeds you sow into Destiny will return as a harvest. The underprivileged child you once mentored may grow up to be the surgeon who is willing to perform the surgery you cannot afford. The computer software you learned to use that wasn't part of your job description may posture you to be hired in a position you would never have qualified for without it.

You may never be cognizant of the price you've paid in some areas, but you may be very clear about others. Write down those that you recognize.

Action   *Harvest*

_____   _____

_____   _____

_____   _____

_____   _____

_____   _____

_____   _____

Why Fight It?

A fight that doesn't lead to a tangible or just end is not worthwhile. You will have some battles in your Destiny journey. There will be obstacles, but you have to choose your skirmishes carefully and know why you're fighting.

Make a list of your major conflicts and consider whether each was a true fight for

Destiny, or if you were simply fighting out of ego or anger or some other emotion. Make an honest assessment of your motive for engaging in the struggle.

The Battle	*The Motivation*
_____	_____
_____	_____
_____	_____
_____	_____
_____	_____
_____	_____

After you have reflected on why and when you have decided to engage in a fight, look at how many of the fights are Destiny driven and which were driven by emotion. If you have engaged in too many conflicts based on ego or emotion, it's time to re-posture your focus and concentrate on the battles that really matter.

Dealing with the Day-to-Day

Author/Poet Dorothy Parker is credited with saying, "I hate writing, I love having written." If you've ever undertaken a writing project, then you understand the truth behind the statement. Completing a book manuscript generates wonderful feelings of accomplishment, but getting there can be an arduous process.

Whatever you dream of becoming, much of the journey to getting there will be tedious, and sometimes even boring. You may not relish every aspect of getting to your journey, but each step is needed to get you there. And when you arrive, you will experience the joy that comes from engaging in the work you know that you were put on earth to do.

Find a special quote or poem or Bible verse that will help inspire you to have patience with the process as you pursue Destiny. Write it here. Write it on a sheet of paper and carry it with you in your wallet or your mobile phone case so that you can look at it whenever you need to for encouragement and affirmation.

_____

_____

_____

_____

_____

Think about someone you know personally who has overcome tremendous odds and obstacles in order to forge a life of meaning and purpose. The person can be older or younger, more educated or less, wealthy or of average means. Ask that person to talk with you about how he or she was able to survive and what were the tools used and the motivation engaged. Your interviewee may name various stimuli that moved him or her to stay in the game, even when times got really, really tough.

You may talk to a mother who fought to provide for her children and stay off welfare after her husband walked away. Perhaps you'll talk to a man who had to use sheer determination to build his business while others relied on social or professional connections. You may even interview an eighteen-year-old athlete whose parents were told he may never overcome the aftereffects of his battle with cancer a decade before.

Write down your takeaway points from the conversation. What does it take to be a champion when the odds are against you?

_____

_____

_____

_____

_____

_____

_____

There's Beauty in Struggle

A butterfly struggles its way out of the cocoon because in the tussle his wings grow strong enough to support his body in flight. A lump of coal endures thousands of years of pressure so it can eventually become a beautiful precious diamond. Before gold can be fashioned into jewelry, it first must endure extreme heat to break it down and shape it into its desired purpose.

Your Destiny journey will involve a series of transformations, evolutions and metamorphoses. Watch this short online video about the Amazing Life Cycle of a Monarch Butterfly (www.youtube.com/watch?v=7AUeM8MbaIk). Produced for the Chicago Nature Museum, the time-lapsed feature shows how the beautiful winged creature evolves from a caterpillar that can fit on the head of a pin to a colorful insect with amazing grace and form.

As you watch the video, think about your own destiny, including your challenges, your growth spurts, your periods of rest and your periods of growth and productivity. When you are done watching, write down some of your most impactful change experiences that were brought to your memory as you watched the butterfly's journey.

_____

_____

_____

_____

_____

_____

The Tough Get Going

Fulfilling a dream takes real work. It takes genuine determination because life gets tough at times. Situations grow complicated and discouraging. You may be tempted to simply give up and choose an easier path.

What is your plan for keeping yourself motivated? Consider these suggestions and check those that best fit you.

- ☐ Listen to an inspiring song that you've adopted as your theme music.
- ☐ Read an inspirational passage or poem or quote.
- ☐ Sit quietly with a lit, scented candle and nourish your dreams by visioning your destiny.
- ☐ Write about your destiny in a journal.
- ☐ Pump up your vision for you future by talking with a confidante or comrade with a positive attitude.
- ☐ Take a walk in nature or look at the stars at night to reconnect to the fact that God has created everything for a purpose, including you.
- ☐ Write down at least a dozen reasons why you should continue pursuing Destiny.
- ☐ Write down at least ten steps you have already taken that have positioned you closer to Destiny.

It's Not What It Looks Like

Think about a situation in your life or in the life of someone you know that didn't turn out like it started. The hobby that began to generate income. The friendship that developed into marriage. The low-level position that positioned you to a greater position at the company.

How did the experience assure you that there is a greater plan for you life?

_____

_____

_____

_____

_____

_____

Sometimes You Have to Duke It Out

Duking it out means a fight, and sometimes you have to do battle and take a stand for Destiny. Are you willing to go into combat, or will you run and hide because the opponent seems too formidable?

Every professional fighter, even a championship pugilist, has strengths and weaknesses. What are your strengths and weaknesses when you have to fight in your life arena? Are you quick to think on your feet? Are you flexible and adjust quickly? Can you keep taking hard hits and refuse to fall? Do you have fancy footwork that helps you dodge peril? Do your knees get weak and want to buckle? Does your heart flutter and send you running for the nearest hiding place?

Write your strengths and weaknesses when you are positioned to have to fight to stay in the game of Destiny. Knowing *how* you fight will help you know how to win the battles you face.

Strengths   *Weaknesses*

_____   _____

_____   _____

_____   _____

_____   _____

_____   _____

Take Care of You

Look at yourself. Look at whether you are caring for your personal needs. Are you taking care of your skin, your dental needs, monitoring your stress level, exercising and eating healthy foods? All of these are ways of taking care of you. It's important because when you get to the top of your destination, you want to be able—mentally, emotionally, physically and spiritually to enjoy the fruit of your journey. But even if you never get to where you hope to be, it's always best to love and take care of yourself.

What are some areas you need to take care of yourself so that you can fully enjoy every aspect of living the life you were destined to have?

_____   _____

_____   _____

_____   _____

_____   _____

Take a Destiny Step

Pray and ask God to reveal your next Destiny step. Commit to your Destiny journey, even if things become challenging. It's no longer time to wait and see. Destiny is calling and now is the time to find the places where your gifts can be used.

Use the space below to write a statement of commitment to God's vision for your future.

_____

_____

_____

_____

_____

_____

CHAPTER 6

✦

Do Your Destiny Thing!

"I think it's good to do your own thing and want to be different, and not look like everyone else."

Alice Dellal

Describe you in 100 words or less. Write as if you are introducing yourself to a crowd that is unfamiliar with your accomplishments. Let the bio reflect how you have done you and made unique contributions to the world around you.

_____

_____

_____

_____

_____

_____

_____

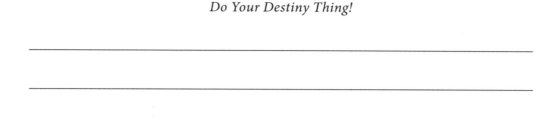

Created to Do You

Saying "Do you!" is a way young people acknowledge each other's right to make personal choices. This sentiment comes from a generation that shuns labels and affirms each other's right to choose the path, the actions or the life choices that seem best. In one way, the phrase implies rebellion against a proscribed way of life, as young people tend to deplore restrictions as they emerge and grow into the space the world opens to accommodate them. But in a very real way, "Do you!" is a good personal philosophy to adopt for establishing the order of your life.

God created you to do you and no one else. Think of all the creative work God put into designing you. Do you think God invested in the creation of humankind out of boredom? You are not an assembly line production. Instead, you were hand fashioned and there will never be another like you. Just think about how you were made.

The intricacies of the human body are simply amazing. Every day your blood travels through over 12,000 miles of blood vessels in your body. God created you for a purpose that unfolds before you as you take the Destiny journey. You are no accident and you are not an assembly line mass production!

What Are Your Personality Distinctives?

Who has your ability to laugh? To mobilize others? To comfort others? To reassure others? To give yourself or someone else a pep talk when feeling down? Write down the things you do like no one else that you know.

Look at yourself in a full length mirror. First look at the features you don't like. Is your hairline receding? Does your nose have a crook in it? Maybe your legs are too long or one is slightly shorter than the other. When we look at models and movie stars, we often think of them as perfect, because that's the image we see on television or in movies and magazines. But they too have flaws that they either conceal or accept as a distinctive feature—a crooked smile, a mole or large ears. Some actors even become famous for their distinctive features. They are no different than you. The difference is, famous people don't let their imperfections stop them from accepting Destiny's invitation, and neither should you.

J.R. Martinez is an actor, best-selling author, motivational speaker, advocate, and wounded U.S. Army veteran. But perhaps most significantly, he is an inspiration because he made the courageous decision to "do you," even after the person he saw in his mirror changed dramatically. In 2002, the El Salvadoran immigrant joined the army and eventually was deployed to Karbala. About a month after his arrival, he hit a roadside bomb and was burned over thirty percent of his body. He has since undergone thirty-four surgeries, including skin grafts and cosmetic surgery. He had always been a handsome young man and easily could have become discouraged about what opportunities lay ahead after the accident.

Martinez did not close the door to Destiny, and as a result his life is radically different from where it began for him as a boy growing up in Hope, Arkansas. A friend encouraged J.R. to audition for an open casting call from the *All My Children* daytime series looking for a veteran. Due to his popularity on the show, the three-month story line for his character developed into a three-year role. Since then he has appeared on numerous television and talk shows. He was featured on the cover of *People* magazine's 2011 *Sexiest Man Alive* issue, and was named one of their Most Intriguing People that same year.

You, too, can embrace your uniqueness as you stay the course of Destiny. Do you, as you and no one else. Think about the features you don't like about yourself.

Then for each one named, list someone successful or famous who has achieved their dream with the same attribute that you perceive as negative, whether it's the sound of your voice, the shape of your legs, the size of hips, your height or a birthmark on your face.

_____   _____

_____   _____

_____   _____

_____   _____

_____   _____

After you review the list, do a bit of research on each of the persons you named. Think about their success and ask, "Why not me?"

Engage yourself in an honest assessment about the unique aspect of yourself that may be fascinating to others. Feel free to brag on yourself. After all, you're talking about a person who's really great!

_____

_____

_____

_____

_____

Get to Know You

You are somebody you'd like to get to know better. Imagine you are a friend or colleague who is about to introduce you to a group and tells them what a capable person you are and why you are someone they should really get to know. What would you say? Practice in the mirror and say it aloud.

Know the Many Facets of You

Are you running from parts of who you are, or have you learned to blend the various parts of you to accept the entire package? Did you have a troubled childhood that you prefer to repress or ignore? Was your lifestyle a bit on the wild side when you were a teenager? Perhaps you've been fired from a couple of jobs as you struggled to find your professional niche.

An important component to navigating your path to Destiny means accepting that every part of you—every experience good or bad—makes you who you are. Embrace the fullness of your life and know that all you went through can serve a purpose, if you allow it to.

Spend some quiet time in a favorite place to think about the parts of your life you need to connect to and realize your personal strength, power and purpose. Maybe you endured painful experiences as a child, but you're still standing today. If you don't already know, spend some time in prayer and meditation. Seek answers from God why you're still here.

Focus on these points:

- ☐ I can't worry about why the past happened.
- ☐ The past is over and I survived it.
- ☐ My past cannot define me or contain me.
- ☐ I am a stronger and better person because I survived.
- ☐ Everything that I've been through makes me unique.
- ☐ Everything I've been through has postured me for my purpose.

Make Peace With It

Are there issues or people from the past that you still regard with anger or shame? Do you have feelings about certain relatives or former associates that you need to resolve?

Circumstances or people from your past may have written your script. It's time to exit stage left and enter a new stage of life. You may be living out a script that says "You're poor and you'll always be poor." And even though you have a very comfortable income, the script is causing you to live like you have very little. You may have watched your mother get hurt by a series of men and you decided long ago that you would never be that vulnerable. So you choose relationships that allow you to be in control, although they are neither healthy nor fulfilling.

List the old scripts that are playing out in your life. After you have written them all down, cross them out, and above them write the new script you want to replace it. For instance your old script may be telling you, "People who've been to college are smarter than I am." Then cross out that script and replace it with a script that God would write for your life to fulfill your destiny, such as: "I am intelligent and knowledgeable and God has equipped me with everything I need.

Old Script:

_____

Old Script:

_____

Old Script:

_____

Old Script:

_____

Celebrate Everyone's Success

Do you make a practice of being happy for people who succeed at something? It's a great way to live because it liberates you from feelings of jealousy, envy and other limiting emotions. Even if you don't necessarily like the person, you can still be happy for him or her. Make a list of people who have recently had a significant accomplishment. Then think about how you can congratulate the person or acknowledge his or her accomplishment—a note, an e-mail or phone call, or even a passing word in the hallway. If you're not able to tell the person directly, reflect on that person's accomplishment with positive thoughts and affirmations.

_____

_____

_____

_____

Signs of Seriousness

What are the signs in your life that you are serious about achieving your destiny?

_____

_____

_____

_____

Destiny Requires Sacrifice

What sacrifices have you made for the sake of your destiny? Have you taken extra classes? Worked two or even three jobs? Taken an unpaid internship? Removed yourself from friendships that were not fruitful? Destiny will not simply fall into your lap. You are expected to invest heavily in your own future. Someone may give you a scholarship, but you have to study and make the grades. You may find an investor, but you have to build the business and provide quality service. How do your actions demonstrate that you are willing to invest in your own destiny?

_____

_____

_____

_____

Make a Contract with Destiny

You already know that Destiny will keep her end and draw every resource possible to help you live your dream. But what about you? Are you as committed to Destiny as she is to you? Write your thoughts. If you need help with this, talk with someone who has been true to his or her vision and get some tips about how to stay committed despite obstacles.

_____

_____

_____

_____

_____

_____

_____

You Are Irreplaceable

Do you really think anyone could ever take your place? Think about the environments where you have the greatest impact—home, work, or in the community. What would each environment be like without you? Draw a dot in each circle that represents the void that would be created without your presence. Make the dot as large as you believe the void would be without you.

Then ask your spouse or someone in your family to do the same exercise concerning you. You may be surprised to discover that your significance in these areas is far greater than you believed.

As you look at the space, remember how valuable you are to the people around you.

   ◯   ◯   ◯

Home   *Work*   *Community*

Take a Destiny Step

Recognize your importance to life. Create a positive statement below that affirms your value to the human race, and then commit it to memory When you're down on yourself, recite those words repeatedly until see the value in yourself once again.

_____

_____

_____

_____

_____

_____

_____

CHAPTER 7

✦

Reset!

"For the past 33 years, I have looked in the mirror every morning and asked myself: 'If today were the last day of my life, would I want to do what I am about to do today?' And whenever the answer has been 'No' for too many days in a row, I know I need to change something."

Steve Jobs

The human brain is such a powerful organ that it can cause us to imagine what does not yet exist. Think about all of the technological gadgets you enjoy on a daily basis. In all likelihood, the majority of them did not exist 40 years ago, or at least in the same form. You enjoy them today because someone first saw it in his or her mind.

The brain's thought capacity can be skewed positively or negatively. We can see great inventions or medical advancements, or we can imagine that everyone we meet is out to do us harm.

There are people who struggle on a daily basis to control their thoughts. For them, thinking positive thoughts or staying on track is challenging. Then there are others who have the power to shift their thinking but they do not because they have been so conditioned to limit what goes on between their ears. Some refuse to allow themselves to stretch their minds to new dimensions.

What are the limiting thoughts, feelings, memories or beliefs that are holding you back from Destiny? It's like living with a chain around your brain, not allowing you to expand to your fullest potential. During slavery, laws were established to prevent enslaved Americans from learning to read or write. Literacy brings exposure and enlightenment, which makes it difficult to keep someone in bondage. The mental bondage served to keep them in physical bondage.

Perhaps a worse form of slavery is confinement of the mind. If your mind is enslaved to small-mindedness, distorted beliefs and fear of the unknown, the path of Destiny becomes cloudy. You could be standing directly in front of your next opportunity but miss it because a chained brain limits your mind.

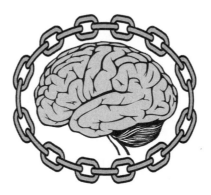

How's the Family?

Part of releasing your mind—and your brainpower—means being aware of family dynamics. For example, you may have grown up in a household that spewed racist dogma without reservation. Perhaps you don't share your family's beliefs, but it's important to consciously step away from those unhealthy dynamics.

When you make the choice to believe differently, then you know that your values are a reflection of your growth and enlightenment, and not simply a rebellious reaction to your family's dysfunctional values.

Making a conscious decision to change your beliefs away from family or generational dynamics also helps you not to fall into an old, negative default mode when you meet with challenges.

What are some ways you have broken away from family default settings that could hinder you from accomplishing your goals and fulfilling your ultimate destiny?

_____

_____

_____

_____

_____

_____

Hit the Reset Button!

Have you ever wished for a life reset button that would allow you to start all over again with certain situations? There are many ways to reset your thinking and impact your life. Look at the various ways explained in the book and determine how you can reset your own life in each category. What would your reset life look like?

Social Reset

_____

_____

_____

Spiritual Reset

_____

_____

_____

Physical Reset

_____

_____

_____

Emotional Reset

_____

_____

_____

Relax Reset

_____

_____

_____

Everything Changes

One thing life teaches us is that normal only stays that way for a period of time. The normal life you had growing up changed as you went from infancy to early childhood to adolescence and eventually to adulthood.

Even after you're all grown up, the normal of your adulthood changes depending on your circumstances. If you married and had children, your normal consisted of constantly caring for someone else's needs, managing the family finances tightly and juggling all of your responsibilities. Your normal became transformed along with your career and economic advancements as well.

You will have many "normals" over your lifetime. Does your level of openness allow you to be flexible enough to accept a new level of "normal" when circumstances change in your life?

Find a song that you like that deals with change or that reminds you of a major change in your life. Listen to it and reflect on the changing stages of your life and how each change has impacted who you are today. Consider how well you've adjusted to the change and whether your receptivity is a barometer of your ability to adapt to new things.

Can You See the Shore?

It's important to see where you're going and the place you want to be must seem attainable or you will give up. Amid foiled plans and broken dreams, seeing your shore will help you to keep moving toward it.

Give yourself the gift of five minutes of visioning your future each day. See yourself as the successful entrepreneur, the student, the newscaster, the singer, the veterinarian, or whatever you hope for as part of your destiny.

In those few minutes, think about what your life will really look like as you are fulfilling Destiny's call. Then you will remember why you're enduring the challenging conditions. Remember, you are not tossing your present life aside for your future. Instead, where you are right now is a part of your evolution to Destiny. Your current circumstances make Destiny all the sweeter because of what you've overcome to get there.

Rain, Rain Go Away!

Nobody likes storms, but somehow through the struggle they make us stronger. Think about the storms you've been through and then consider how your endurance through them has benefitted you.

The Storm   *The Benefit*

_____   _____

Reset!

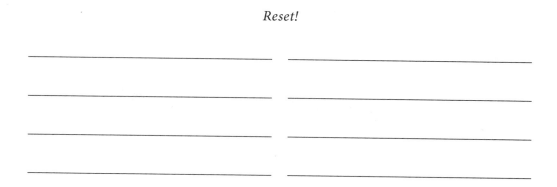

I Can See Clearly Now, the Rain Is Gone

Think about a storm you endured that felt very lonely, yet afterward, you realized the presence of God was with you all along.

Read the "Footprints in the Sand" poem written in 1936 by Mary Stevenson and think about how God carried you when you couldn't see your own way.

"Footprints in the Sand"
One night I dreamed I was walking along the beach with the Lord.
Many scenes from my life flashed across the sky.
In each scene I noticed footprints in the sand.
Sometimes there were two sets of footprints,
other times there were one set of footprints.

This bothered me because I noticed
that during the low periods of my life,
when I was suffering from
anguish, sorrow or defeat,
I could see only one set of footprints.

So I said to the Lord,
"You promised me Lord,
that if I followed you,
you would walk with me always.
But I have noticed that during
the most trying periods of my life

65

there have only been one
set of footprints in the sand.
Why, when I needed you most,
you have not been there for me?"

The Lord replied,
"The times when you have
seen only one set of footprints,
is when I carried you."

Mary Stevenson

It feels good to come out of a storm. Think about some of the storms you've come through as you listen to the song "I Can See Clearly Now," by either Jimmy Cliff or Johnny Nash. Both versions are available online. Take a moment to revel in the joy of passed storms and remember them as confirmation that you will make it through future storms also.

By Faith or By Sight?

There is a difference between living and acting according to what we can see versus what we believe by faith. Many times human beings have a difficult time operating according to their faith—whether their faith is in God, or in the power of Destiny's draw.

We tend to trust what we can touch and see rather than what we can believe or intuit. Which mode do you operate in most often and why?

_____

_____

_____

_____

_____

Tracking Your Normal

Think about some of the mile marker years of your life—ages 18, 25 30, 40, 50, 60, 65 and so forth. What was the normal for that time in your life? Keep going until you reach your current age.

At 18, you were probably about to finish high school and your days consisted of hanging out with friends, going to class and perhaps working a part-time job. At age 25, you may have been taking your profession seriously, or trying to figure it out. You may have been planning to marry.

Write down your normal for those ages and think about how your life has changed. Think about the skills and tools you engaged to switch from one normal to another. How were you able to adapt to each new normal? Then consider how your life will continue to change.

Age_____

_____

_____

_____

Age_____

_____

_____

_____

Age_____

_____

_____

Age_____

_____

_____

_____

Age_____

_____

_____

_____

Age_____

_____

_____

_____

Age_____

_____

_____

_____

Now imagine what your normal will look like during your next mile marker year, and the one after that.

Age_____

_____

_____

_____

Age_____

_____

_____

_____

Maybe It's Time to Change Your Tune

It's been said that relationships are like a dance. It takes two people moving in sync to the same beat. The problem may come when you began moving to the beat of your destiny while others are moving to whatever beat that appeals to them or that is offered to them.

Think about the times you've changed partners in your life dance. Who have you had to walk away from on the dance floor? In what situations have you had to stop the music because you no longer wanted to dance to that beat?

What was the new music you began dancing to after you walked away?

Old Music (people or situations)   *New Music (change in the direction of Destiny)*

_____   _____

_____   _____

_____   _____

_____   _____

_____   _____

Take a Destiny Step

Prioritize finding your authentic self, which includes your gifts and your desires. Answer the question posed at the beginning of the chapter, "Who am I, really?"

_____

_____

_____

_____

_____

_____

_____

CHAPTER 8

✤

Don't Waste a Minute

"You will never change your life until you change something you do daily. The secret of your success is found in your daily routine."

John C. Maxwell

Time is your greatest asset, if used properly. Your time is worth everything because it is not a renewable resource.

Dr. Benjamin Elijah Mays served as president of Morehouse College from 1940 to 1967. In those twenty-seven years he committed to memory a poem to teach students at the elite all-male institution about the value of time. Even today, if you talk to a man who went to Morehouse during the years of Mays' tenure, most likely, he can still recite this poem.

God's Minute

I've only just a minute,
Only sixty seconds in it.
Forced upon me, can't refuse it,
Didn't seek it, didn't choose it,
But it's up to me to use it.
I must suffer if I lose it,
Give an account if I abuse it,
Just a tiny little minute,
But eternity is in it.

After you've read the poem a couple of times think about importance of every single minute you've been given to your destiny. Then think about how you can reset your thinking about time and take advantage of every minute of this priceless resource God has given you.

Has Your Youth Gone to Waste?

Irish writer George Bernard Shaw stated, "Youth is wasted on the young." That's a statement that's best understood after we've lived awhile, made some mistakes, wasted some time and lost some dreams.

As the number of years we've lived begins to add up, we realize what we possessed during our years of youthful idealism and vigor.

As you consider your own Destiny journey, how does Shaw's statement apply to your life? Have you wasted youthful energy and enthusiasm? Have you grown suspicious and less hopeful as you've experienced disappointments?

_____

_____

_____

_____

_____

_____

_____

_____

Countdown

Living with optimism that it's never too late for something to happen is a great personal philosophy. But the reality that time waits for no one is an ever-present reality. Medical science has made some amazing advances, but generally, a woman can't wait until she's fifty before she starts planning to get pregnant. A man wanting to be a professional athlete can't start at age fifty. Some moments must be seized before it's too late.

Only God knows how much longer you will live, but think about this. If you live to be age eighty-five, how much time do you have left to accomplish the things you want to do? How many days do you have? If you're age fifty right now, that means you have over twelve thousand days left. It may seem like a lot of days, but is it really? You will spend almost a third of those days sleeping, and certainly no less than a fourth. If you sleep six hours per night, then you will spend almost thirty-two hundred days sleeping. You will spend over 100 days eating. You have to factor in the equivalent of days spent driving, showering, getting dressed, mowing the lawn, house cleaning, exercising, and so forth. After you've roughly totaled these days, how many do you really have left for living your dream?

British author William Penn once said, *"Time is what we want most, but what we use worst."* You may think you're wasting time doing some activities, when in reality they may not be the real time drains in your life. How much time do you spend surfing the Internet, chatting on social media or hanging out socializing? Are you "killing" the time that could better be used investing in your destiny?

How Do You Tend to "Kill" Your Time?

_____

_____

_____

_____

_____

_____

_____

_____

Now, does it still seem like you have a lot of time left to accomplish what you desire? And, as you are able to accomplish the things you want, you like to have the physical and mental agility to enjoy the pursuit of those endeavors.

What if those days were dollars? It doesn't take long to spend $365. It doesn't take long to spend $12,000.00. And just like money can slip through your fingers before you know it, so can your time. As you age, you begin to wonder, "Where did the time go?"

What are some ways you allow time to slip away from you? You can take control of your time, just as you take control of your financial resources. Write down some of the ways time slips away—some might include gossiping about or prying into what others are doing, excessive sleeping, being afraid, watching extreme amounts of television, mindlessly surfing the Internet, substance abuse.

Do you value your time? Based on your daily activity, rate how much your time is worth to you.

No Value	Some Value	Priceless	Priceless
I spend lots of time engaged in activities unrelated to my destiny.	I go along with whatever the day brings.	I plan some activities but wait for others to happen	I make good use of every moment

Lessons on Time

What life lessons have helped you to understand the value of time? Losing someone we love often can be the catalyst that causes us to reflect on the fact that life is finite and shifts us to begin prioritizing how we use the days, hours, weeks and months we are given. Sometimes it's watching employees who were hired after you being promoted over you. Or it may be reading the obituary of someone who has died, but yet never really lived. How are you learning to value time?

_____

_____

_____

_____

_____

_____

_____

_____

_____

_____

You Can't Hurry Destiny

Resisting the urge to push Destiny along can be tempting, especially when others seem to be briskly moving along their own course of life. It's good to take an occasional assessment of your life and how you're using your time, but it is equally important to stay on track with your authentic journey.

If you're trying to hurry Destiny, you can push yourself to move fast, perhaps faster than you're ready. When that happens, your life can begin to feel out of control, much like driving a car at a high rate of speed.

If you have a smartphone or tablet, download a free car racing app and begin to drive it faster than you can manage. What will happen? Before long, you'll crash because your skill level at the game was no match for the speed at which the race car could travel.

You don't want your life to crash, so it's important to be honest with yourself regarding the pace at which you are moving toward Destiny. As hard as it may be to be patient, you simply have to trust that God is in control of your speed. Give God the wheel of your race car to ensure that you will not crash and burn while on the ride.

It's Worth the Wait

Your Destiny is worth waiting for, because you don't want to push and rush yourself into a life that really doesn't belong to you. What are some things you once wished or prayed would happen fast, but later were glad that it was delayed or never happened?

_____

_____

_____

_____

_____

_____

Cherish the Moments

You've had some special moments that have played an important role in your destiny. Think about those events—how you chose your college major, meeting your future employer, meeting your business partner or spouse, having your first child, or finding your first home.

Make a list of the circumstances in your life that you later recognized as Destiny moments. You couldn't see it then, but as you reflect, you likely can appreciate how special those times were.

As you reminisce, consider that Destiny will place you in many situations that are not chance nor are they coincidence. They simply are confirmation that God has a plan for your life.

_____

_____

_____

_____

_____

_____

_____

_____

_____

_____

_____

_____

_____

_____

_____

_____

_____

Everything Must Change

You've probably heard someone talk about how great things used to be. It's true that every element of the past has great merits. But there are many present-day assets, too. With each change in your personal life, in society, in the political or social landscape, you've had to adjust with it.

Depending on your age, you may remember the days before cable television, satellite radio, Internet and smartphones.

If you have kept pace with the technological changes of society, you've had to make some personal adjustments.

You also may have made psychological shifts in how you feel about certain social practices, about racial issues, or about certain medical procedures.

What are some of the major changes you've kept in touch with over the past 20 years. It's important to stay in touch because the further behind you are, the further behind you will stay, because life will continue to move on. Whether you like the changes or not, staying aware of societal shifts helps you to keep pace. Place a check mark by the things you kept track of.

- ☐ Personal Computers
- ☐ Tablets
- ☐ Social media
- ☐ Smart TVs
- ☐ Smartphones
- ☐ Political Campaigns
- ☐ Views on religion
- ☐ Medical Ethics
- ☐ Racial Demographics

Don't Write Your Destiny Off

Destiny has no age limit. Only you can restrict your destiny by telling yourself you're too old or that it's too late.

What are the things you've determined you're too old to do? If there's something you believe you're too old to do, it's almost certain that you can find a story about someone who has done that same thing at your age or even older.

What are you too old to do?

_____

_____

_____

_____

_____

_____

_____

_____

Now, name someone your age who has done it:

_____

_____

_____

_____

_____

_____

Just like you probably found someone older than you, it's highly probable that someone younger than you has already accomplished what you are trying to do. How can you remain focused on your own journey and keep going, even though there may be someone young enough to be your child doing the same thing?

In 1974, ten-year-old Tatum O'Neal earned an Academy Award as Best Supporting Actress for *Paper Moon*. She remains the youngest actor to ever receive the prestigious Oscar. At age eighty-two, Christopher Plummer earned an Oscar in 2012 for his performance in *Beginners*. Was Plummer's achievement any less significant than O'Neal's? Should he not have strived to give the greatest performance he could because Hollywood's top honor was once given to a ten-year-old girl?

Why should you keep moving toward your destiny, even though others far younger than you have made similar accomplishments?

The Days of Our Lives

You may not have accomplished all that you hope to do, but more than likely you have made some strides of which you are, and should be, proud.

Write down some of your achievements, as well as things you hope to do. After you complete the exercise, you should have an objective look at how you have used the days you have been given.

Things done well	*Things not yet accomplished*
_____	_____
_____	_____
_____	_____
_____	_____
_____	_____
_____	_____
_____	_____
_____	_____

Take a Destiny Step

Answer the question, If I continue to spend my time as I do currently, what is the likelihood that I will accomplish my destiny?

_____

_____

_____

_____

_____

_____

CHAPTER 9

✦

Connect the Dots of Your Destiny!

> "Creativity itself doesn't care at all about results the only thing it craves is the process. Learn to love the process and let whatever happens next happen, without fussing too much about it. Work like a monk, or a mule, or some other representative metaphor for diligence. Love the work. Destiny will do what it wants with you, regardless."
>
> *Elizabeth Gilbert*

Watching someone throw away a gift is a sad sight. Imagine watching a father give his son a Rolex watch for graduation and the son throws it in the garbage. What if you saw a mother give her daughter a pearl necklace that belonged to the girl's grandmother, but instead of wearing them she threw them in a bottle of bleach? No doubt, you would shake your head and respond, "Aw, what a shame!"

Some respond the same way to gifts they have been given by God. The United Negro College Fund adopted the phrase, "A mind is a terrible thing to waste," to encourage support for education through scholarships. Indeed, wasting your mind can have disastrous consequences. Watching a young man with a brilliant IQ fry his brain smoking crystal meth is heartbreaking. Listening to a middle-aged woman make excuses for not going after her dream is discouraging. Yet God watches us each day as we toss aside the gifts we have been given. We discard them out of fear, out of ignorance or out of ingratitude.

The brilliant and witty newspaper columnist Erma Bombeck is quoted as saying,

"When I stand before God at the end of my life, I would hope that I would not have a single bit of talent left, and could say, 'I used everything you gave me.'"

Isn't that a wonderful resolution to make? Imagine living in the knowledge that you have used everything God has given you to improve your life or someone else's.

What are your unused gifts? How can you reclaim them and use them? Even the seemingly insignificant gifts are important to use. You may be a successful surgeon who has neglected her gift for refinishing furniture. You may not need to restore your own furniture, but you could use that gift to help someone else, and perhaps help yourself experience a measure of fulfillment in the process.

Unused Gift	*How you can use it*

_____   _____

                                           _____

                                           _____

                                           _____

Do you allow yourself the pleasure of dreaming since you've become an adult? You can't dream your life away, but it's important not to lose the ability to envision something for yourself. Children are wonderfully imaginative and creative. But often as we grow older, we regard limitless thinking as childish or unrealistic.

Give yourself five minutes a day as you read this chapter to simply dream about the better life that you want—better housing, a better career, a better physique, a better relationship. Keep the vision in your head and your heart, and then write down what that looks like.

Stay Focused on Destiny

Most of us are easily distracted, even from the things we want most in life. Not every disruption to your vision can be avoided, but it's important to distinguish the life interruptions that can be dismissed from those that can be pushed aside.

Use the space below to determine the kinds of distractions that require your attention from those that you can ignore.

Essential Distractions	*Unnecessary Distractions*
_____	_____
_____	_____
_____	_____
_____	_____
_____	_____

Give Yourself a Talk

What's the self-talk that equips you to ignore a situation, as if you were wearing blinders? Write your own speech below that encourages you to stay focused and ignore issues unrelated to your destiny:

_____

_____

_____

_____

_____

_____

_____

Find Value in Diversity

Have you limited yourself to a comfort zone of people who look like you, think like you, eat the same foods you do and live in the same neighborhood? It's amazing that so many people are comfortable living in a limited existence, never being exposed to the richness of diversity. It begs the question, How many people have blocked Destiny because they refuse to open their minds beyond the familiar?

Do some online, library or on-site exploration of a culture that is not yours and one with which you are not familiar. Often various cultural or ethnic groups will sponsor community or street festivals that celebrate various aspects of their heritage.

Visit a cultural street festival or spend some time socializing with people who are not in your usual social circle. Learn with an open mind and allow yourself to be fascinated by different languages, foods, familial relationships and holidays. Use the experience to gain an appreciation for God's broad design of humanity.

The Joneses Aren't Real

"Keeping up with the Joneses," means trying to compete with people in the attainment of material goods or social achievements. Think about the decisions you've made that amounted to little more that a competitive acquisition—a car, a relationship, or even a degree. These kinds of accomplishments are some of the most unrewarding we can undertake.

Write down some of your endeavors, whether something you purchased or something you worked to attain. Circle those that caused you to really feel good about yourself. You might really feel good to have been the first in your family to attend college. Or you may have felt good to be able to purchase your first new car.

Then write a J next to those that were acquired to keep up with the Joneses. Think about whether the competitive achievements were worth the effort it took to get them, and remember that the things done out of a true sense of purpose or passion are the most fulfilling.

_____   _____

_____   _____

_____   _____

_____   _____

_____   _____

What's Your SCQ (Street Cred Quotient)?

By virtue of your experiences, you've gained knowledge and skill in certain areas. The abilities and exposure you have acquired give you "street cred" in certain components of your life. If you've raised children as a single father, you have street cred to share with others on the matter. If you established a growing business from a corner of your home basement, you have the authority to share with others who are seeking such opportunities.

Write down the areas you have street cred. Then think about how what you've earned can be helpful to others. Then make the final connection how helping others with valuable information and expertise can help position you toward your destiny.

My Street Cred	*Can help others by...*

It's Complicated...

Life can be complicated, and charting the path to Destiny can confound matters even further. What are some of the complications of your life, the things you feel others may not understand or readily accept about you?

Look at yourself in the mirror. Then use an erasable marker or lipstick to write on the complicated parts of your life. Divorce? Incest? Flunking out? Alcoholism? Welfare? Bankruptcy? As you write down each issue, draw an arrow from that issue to your face. Look at the issues and then look at you. Think about how each of those complex issues has helped to shape you into the person you are today. If you can't use a mirror, use a picture of yourself or a photocopy of your image.

As you reflect on the issues, think about how you can own those issues and put them in proper perspective, and perhaps even be grateful for them because they have impacted who you are today.

Ordinary Breeds Extraordinary

God writes the script that prepares us to do what he has assigned to us. Your life story probably includes some relatively common experiences that shaped who you are and influenced how you are able to do what you do. For example, many famous rappers were influenced by the urban poverty of their neighborhoods where they grew up. You may be a person who entered the medical field after taking care of an elderly grandparent. Or perhaps the teacher who believed in you propelled you to work harder and it changed your life.

Recall and write down an experience from your life that was ordinary, but yet had an extraordinary impact on your life. Describe how you were affected by it. Then think about how you can begin to look for special outcomes from the everyday occurrences in your life.

_____

_____

_____

_____

_____

_____

_____

Thanks, Trouble!

Problematic times and difficult people can wreak havoc on your life, but the troubles they cause you to grow stronger, be wiser and better informed. Think of two particularly painful situations that resulted in you becoming better in some way. Write the person or circumstance a thank-you note that, despite what you went through you have become a more powerful, confident, and capable person. Purchase an inexpensive package of thank-you notes from the dollar store and write out as many notes that you need for your experiences.

Certified

What is the value of the education you have gotten outside of any classroom? You've learned some things and graduated in some areas and deserve to be recognized for your accomplishments.

Make copies of the diploma below and complete one for yourself in every area where you have gained life-altering knowledge. If you've gained survival skills from being betrayed, from relationships gone bad or from various professional experiences, acknowledge what you've gained from those circumstances.

Display your diplomas if you like, or place them in a portfolio.

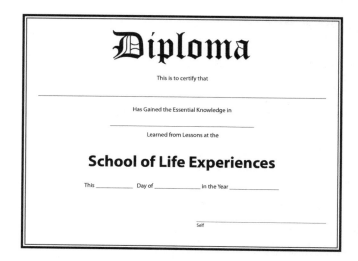

Your Destiny Blocks

Your experiences build on each other. Fill in the bricks below, thinking about how your employment, relationship, financial or other experiences have built upon each other and taken you to higher and higher levels.

You Will Find Your Way

Your life may sometimes feel like a maze, going through route after route, only to hit dead end walls. Getting to your destination can be complicated. Work through the maze below while thinking of your own challenges that you've navigated through.

My Life Without Struggle

Take about thirty minutes of quiet time to reflect on who you might have become if you had never struggled. How did the struggle build your character? Make a list of who you are because of struggle and who you might have become without struggle.

Without Struggle	*Because of Struggle*
_____	_____
_____	_____
_____	_____
_____	_____
_____	_____

Whether you are a spiritual person or not, trusting God with your destiny is a challenge. Think about the struggles and experiences you wrote about in the above exercise. Did the experience inspire trust in God or cause you to believe you have only yourself to rely upon.

Use the sign below to remind you to relax and trust God with your destiny. As you look at the sign, think about what you will do if you don't trust God. What's your alternative to trusting God?

Provisions

One of our greatest struggles may be believing that we will have what we need to accomplish what we desire to do. Very often our vision to recognize the resources we already have is polluted by our fears and doubts. Sometimes what we seek is already in our possession; we simply fail to realize it.

You may need a college degree to accomplish your vision, but you're hindered by a lack of resources. Draw internally. You may be limiting yourself because you can't afford tuition, but haven't bothered to look for scholarships offered for people in your circumstances. If you searched, you may be amazed to find there is scholarship money available for an electrician who wants to major in computer software development.

Even when you don't have what you need, that doesn't preclude you from asking God for it. Ask God for what you need to fulfill your destiny. After all, God crafted the destiny for you, so doesn't it seem reasonable that you can rely on some divine assistance to get you there?

What Do You Need?

Write down what you think you need to move a step closer to your destiny. Then pray over those needed provisions and trust that God will make them available to you. Keep your eyes open. Look for them to come. They may not appear when you expect, but God will position you to receive them when the time is right.

_____ _____

_____ _____

_____ _____

_____ _____

_____ _____

Can You Trust God?

Can you trust God enough to do a spiritual trust fall into God's arms as you trust God with your destiny? Think about where you want to do you. What are your dreams? As you hold on to that image mentally, imagine yourself doing a free fall into God's arms. Are you ready to trust the Almighty, or would you resist and prefer to trust your own abilities?

We've all been a guest who refused to leave one of life's parties. A relationship, a job, a financial encumbrance, can cause us to hang on much too long. What did you hang onto long after you should have let go or walked away? How did your refusal to release the circumstance affect you and your destiny? Write your thoughts below.

_____

_____

_____

_____

_____

_____

_____

_____

_____

_____

_____

_____

Take a Destiny Step

Write down what you think you need to move a step closer to your destiny. Then pray or meditate over those needed provisions and trust that God will make them available to you. Keep your eyes open. Look for them to come. They may not appear when you expect, but God will position you to receive them when the time is right.

_____   _____

_____   _____

_____   _____

_____   _____

_____   _____

CHAPTER 10

✦

Getting Unstuck

"Any action is often better than no action, especially if you have been stuck in an unhappy situation for a long time. If it is a mistake, at least you learn something, in which case it's no longer a mistake. If you remain stuck, you learn nothing."

Eckhart Tolle

We are all trying to grow and move and change for the better. We strive for more education, better health, career advancement, to conceive or rear children, to acquire better opportunities, or better living conditions for our family. The reality is change does not always come easy; but it is attainable. In our efforts to move forward we can instead feel stuck.

You can be stymied by your career, your relationships, finances, educational level, emotions, your past, physical abilities, or even the routines of life. Those feelings are not uncommon, but if you're feeling stuck, it's important to recognize that you still have many things already in your favor.

If you stay in a mode of feeling trapped, it may be hard to feel hopeful and see potential for change around you. It's important to feel that you are a person of immense possibilities, despite your immediate circumstances.

First, acknowledge the place where you're feeling stuck and complete the following sentence:

The place where I feel stuck is _____. The reason why I feel stuck is _____

_____

_____

_____.

After you complete the sentence, think about the place were you feel stymied. If it's a physical location, such as your house or job, look around and conduct an assessment of the positive aspects. For instance, if you are feeling stuck on your job, look around your place of employment and look for the positive aspects of your job. What benefits do you gain from your job? Look for hopeful signs that things can change and write them down.

_____

_____

_____

_____

_____

Make a list of ten accomplishments that you would expect from a person who is successful.

_____   _____

_____   _____

_____   _____

_____   _____

_____   _____

Recognize Your Success

You may be more successful than you think. How will you know unless you make an assessment? You may be struggling to make mortgage payments, but if you own a home, that makes you successful. The place where you've worked for 20 years may feel stifling, but the fact that you've held employment at the same place for an extended period makes you successful. Having a stable income for twenty years counts as a successful accomplishment.

Despite the challenges at home, work or in other aspects of your life, draw out the aspects that remind you of your positive achievements. Write down five accomplishments you have made based on the list you created in the last exercise.

_____

_____

_____

_____

_____

Shake It Off!

Sometimes you have to shake things off, just like the donkey in the illustration used in the book. Sometimes all you need is a few simple words of wisdom to encourage you to remember to move past the issue. Find a quote from a respected person or from an online search or a Bible verse that will encourage you to let go of old, useless feelings, resentments and issues that can keep you stuck in an unhealthy place. Write your quote here and also keep it with you at all times—in a wallet, phone case, etc.

_____

_____

_____

_____

See the Changes in You

Time changes things and people. How you handle something today is probably quite different from how you would have addressed the issue twenty-five years ago.

Think about the ways you've grown, beyond physically, that have taught you to respond to issues differently today than you would just ten years ago.

_____

_____

_____

_____

_____

_____

_____

Meet the Warrior Inside of You

The Warrior Spirit in you will not be denied. The key is to get in touch with the fighting spirit inside of you and make it work for you. Your Warrior Spirit has a purpose—to help you win in life. Get in touch with who your Warrior Spirit is by figuring out his or her traits. Think about the fighter in you. What moves him to fight? What gets her angry? What weapons does he use to fight? How long is she willing to fight?

Get in touch with your Warrior Spirit by writing a description here:

_____

_____

_____

_____

_____

_____

Strength or Weakness?

Make a list of your strengths in one column. In an adjacent column, list how those strengths can become weaknesses if not kept in check.

Strengths Kept	*Strong Strengths Made Weak*
_____	_____
_____	_____
_____	_____
_____	_____

God Is Your Partner

We live and operate in a divine-human partnership. We have been given an earthly assignment by God, but it is up to us to choose to fulfill that task. Therefore, God and human beings work together in partnership. What does your arrangement with God look like? What is God's commitment to the agreement? What is your commitment to it?

God's Part   *My Part*

_____   _____

_____   _____

_____   _____

_____   _____

Is Destiny Waiting for You to Move?

Have you ever tried to help someone get access onto a busy street in the middle of rush-hour traffic? You pause to give them a second to enter, but they won't seize the moment. You can see it in their eyes. They want to come out into traffic, but they're waiting for conditions all around them to be perfect before jumping out there. It's as if they expect everyone to stop and give them time to enter the street at an easy, relaxed pace.

There may be people trying to help you, maybe even God is trying to help you, but you're stuck because you're waiting on conditions all around you to be perfect before you jump in. You may have to dive into you next opportunity, even though you already feel like you don't have enough hours in the day to do it all. You may live on three or four hours' sleep for a time. You may brown-bag it to lunch every day for a while.

Destiny will never require you to be foolhardy, but you may have to take some steps that might appear a little crazy to the rest of the world.

Find some quiet time to really think about whether or not you have what you need to make a move. You may only be able to nudge a bit further, but that's still closer to where you want to be.

Turn on some music that is peaceful to you and create a meditation time to reflect on what it means to have the audacity to have optimism about achieving your destiny.

Take a Destiny Step

Think about what you're really waiting for. Meditate on this statement and share your thoughts here: "Who's waiting on whom? Am I waiting on God, or is God waiting on me?"

_____

_____

_____

_____

CHAPTER 11

✦

Seek Wise Counsel

"What you want in a mentor is someone who truly cares for you and who will look after your interests and not just their own. When you do come across the right person to mentor you, start by showing them that the time they spend with you is worthwhile."

Vivek Wadhwa

Talent is never enough to get you to Destiny. Having exceptional abilities may get you in the door or where you want to be, but it won't keep you there. Many gifted celebrities, professional athletes and corporate heads have reached the top of their game, only to tumble because there was no one to advise them. The problem wasn't their level of giftedness. They lacked something even more important.

No matter how gifted we are when we are born, we all need teachers, helpers, counselors and guides through various stages of our life journey. Over our lifetime, there likely will be many such persons. Even if we reach the pinnacle of Destiny's invitation to us, we still will need counsel or advice on occasion.

Who are the people you know that live fully, who are successful in their profession, in their homes, in their relationships with others and have good self-esteem? People like this are great mentors and are the kind of people worth developing mentor-mentee relationships with.

Find the best advisors and counselors available to you, but just remember one important thing. The best advice in the world is rendered no good if you are not willing to listen to it. Before seeking a mentor, think about whether you are ready to be mentored.

Who Was There For You?

Your mentors may come and go, depending on the challenges you face at certain times in your life. Your mentor in high school may have been a teacher, athletic coach or school counselor. In college, it may have been a professor or local business/community leader. Your mentor on your first job may have been an experienced co-worker or business owner.

Think about your greatest periods of challenge on the time line below. Write them on the time line and underneath, write down the name of the person or group that was there to support or mentor you through it.

Event: _____

Supporters: _____

Event: _____

Supporters: _____

Event: _____

Supporters: _____

Reflect on how the people you needed came into your life. Think about how God sent the support you needed at just the right time.

If you do not currently have a mentor, trust that God will send who you need at the time you are ready to receive his or her guidance. The right relationship will form. The proper alliance will develop.

Can You Handle the Truth?

Think about whether you are really ready to have a mentor. Can you stand someone giving you an honest critique of the choices you make regarding your career or any other component of your destiny? Would you be offended by someone suggesting that you change the way you dress? How about an honest appraisal of your grammar? Can you handle someone telling you to work out or go to the dentist, if physical appearance is critical to your job?

Will you look at the guidance of a mentor as a sincere effort to help you improve and come closer to your destiny? Or will your ego get in the way and cause you to back away from an effective mentor who's not afraid to be honest with you?

List the qualities you think an effective mentor should have. Feel free to look for some online articles on mentoring to help you create this list. Then, next to each characteristic, place a check mark by those traits you are ready to handle from an advisor. Place an x next to those you know you are not ready to deal with.

_____   _____

_____   _____

_____   _____

_____   _____

_____   _____

_____   _____

Look at the mentor characteristics you are not yet ready to handle. How does your perspective need to change in order to be ready for the best mentor you can get?

Are You a Bootstrap Person?

Answer these six questions:

1. Do you often refuse help when offered?
2. Do you tend to resolve your problems in silence and isolation?
3. Do you believe you can't depend on anyone else?
4. Do you believe no one else wants to or is willing to help you?
5. Do you dread feeling like you owe someone for having helped you?
6. Do you take pride in having accomplished something all alone?

If you answered yes to some of these questions, you may be a bootstrap kind of person. But consider this. Yes, independence certainly has its merits, but it is delusional to believe you will never need the help of another person. Also, when you refuse the aid of others, you cheat them out of the joy of contributing to someone else's life. Allow someone to have the pleasure of investing in you because you are worth it! Then, when you are operating in your destiny, you will have an opportunity to experience that same joy by helping someone else.

Do You Need a Mentor?

Sometimes people do not recognize that they need mentoring. Having a trusted, experienced advisor is not just for the young or for the novice. Mentors can be beneficial to your life at any age or stage.

Think about what a mentor can help you to do at this point in your life by identifying what you need and then try to match that with who can help provide that for you.

Need	*Possible Mentor*
_____	_____
_____	_____
_____	_____
_____	_____
_____	_____

Identify your most intense need, and then try to determine how to establish a relationship with the person who can give you guidance to get to the next level of where you want to go.

_____

_____

_____

_____

_____

_____

Are You Properly Positioned?

We have to be in the right places to attract the kind of mentors we need. You don't just need to be in the right physical location, but also the right mental and spiritual place as well. You won't attract a powerful mentor by hanging around people who have no goals. When your head and spirit are in the right place, you'll have no desire to be around those who can only drag you down. Worthy mentors are priceless commodities who don't have time to waste.

Think about where you spend most of your time. Are you properly positioned to connect with a strong mentor? List the places where you spend most of your time. If you are not spending time in the places where a good mentor might be, think about how you can expose yourself to greater opportunities.

For example, if all of your time is spent working, watching television and sleeping, you can hardly expect to bond with a strong mentor. Of course you need to work, but perhaps your lunch hour could be spent near the company of people who can advise you properly. Look at your schedule and figure out how you can invest some time more wisely to position you where you want and need to be.

Daily Activity	*Alternative Activity*
_____	_____
_____	_____

_____   _____

_____   _____

_____   _____

Do You Ask, Seek and Knock?

Think about how this principle can help you find a mentor. How can you engage such a person? Who would you most like to mentor you? If you found a way to associate with him or her, how would you make a connection using the ask, seek, knock principle?

Consider whether you are genuinely interested in that person's life, or are you only concerned about what they can do for you?

Get your O-J-T

Education and training are essential, but so is practical experience. How can you gain on-the-job training to help position you for Destiny? Ask yourself some critical questions.

- ☐ Are you willing to set your ego aside and engage in some seemingly menial tasks?
- ☐ Are you ready to listen to the sage advice of a mentor who may suggest a job you never considered?
- ☐ Are your feelings easily hurt, or do you have a tough skin for honest feedback?
- ☐ Are you willing to work for free or even pay your own way to get the kind of OJT you need?

Step into a New Circle

Imagine you have an opportunity to be in a circle of the highest ranking people in your field of endeavor. How might you handle the situation?

- ☐ Can you give up status and be humble in a room full of highly accomplished people?
- ☐ Will you embellish your accomplishments to pretend you know as much as they or that you are equally as experienced?
- ☐ Will you be tempted to dismiss some of the experts because they don't fit the profile of what you think they should look or sound like? What if you want to be mentored in the fashion industry, but one of the greatest mentors you could have is overweight and never attempts to fit into the clothing trends touted?
- ☐ Can you enter the circle with an open mind, much like a blank tablet, ready for an entirely new script?
- ☐ Can you separate nonessentials? If the person who can best mentor you in an industry has a personal habit or lifestyle that is contrary to your choices, would you still be open to a mentoring relationship?
- ☐ Could you be trusted to use discretion regarding telling others about the information gained and people you met, or could you not resist the urge to name-drop to others?

As you answer the questions, think about whether you are truly ready for a new circle of associations. As you become ready, the opportunities will present themselves.

Take a Destiny Step

Write down the names of people who may be willing to serve as your mentor. Then write down a deadline date to ask the person to serve in that capacity.

_____   _____

_____   _____

_____   _____

_____   _____

_____   _____

CHAPTER 12

✦

Failure Isn't Always Bad

"Failure is the opportunity to begin again more intelligently."

Henry Ford

Failure is painful and embarrassing...because we associate a failed deed with a failed self. We go to great lengths to avoid the appearance of failure. But must failure always be bad? At some point, life requires that we get off the merry-go-round of perfectionism and realize failure is not a bad thing; it is a growing thing.

If failure were all bad, then many successful people would have given up long before the attainment of their dream. Many people who are now highly successful have failed in business many times, or have even gone bankrupt before achieving financial success.

What is your definition of success and failure? What do you think is God's definition of failure? Do you define them differently? Can anything good come out of the failures that you've experienced?

Who's Who Today

If you have your high school yearbook, go back and look at it. Who were the people voted most likely to succeed? Did they? Sometimes the graduates considered to have the most potential for success don't, while people who are overlooked can go on to have great accomplishments.

What were the qualities of those who succeeded but never got voted among the superlatives by classmates? What made those voted in appear to have what it takes to be successful to other teenagers? Would you still consider those attributes necessary for success today?

_____

_____

_____

_____

_____

_____

Take an Honest Look at You

Have you ever pretended to be more successful at something than you really are? Perhaps you've given the impression that your job, your lifestyle or your marriage is something that it's not in order to make other people have a certain image of you.

What feelings motivated you to give a less than honest impression of yourself?

_____

_____

_____

How did you feel while you were portraying a better image of yourself?

_____

_____

How would you have felt had you simply told the truth about your circumstances?

_____

_____

_____

How Has Failure Helped You?

Think of the three major failures you've experienced. What was the most painful loss coming from that failure? How much did feelings like shame, anger and defeat play a role in how the failure was perceived?

_____

_____

_____

Complete this sentence:

My biggest failure caused me to feel _____ because I (lost/no longer/can't)_____
_____.

Were you able to find redemption in your failure? Did anything good come from it?

_____

_____

_____

What were the questions you asked God in the aftermath of your failure?

_____

_____

_____

Are You All In?

Consider what it would mean for you to have "all in" determination in your life, where you risk everything and go for Destiny with nothing held back. What would you do?

_____

_____

_____

_____

_____

_____

Safe Success

Now think of what a "safe succeed" life would look like. What career/lifestyle do you choose if you want to do something that's guaranteed not to fail as it required no risk?

_____

_____

_____

_____

_____

_____

Failure Is Opportunity

There's a saying that when you're down, there's no place to go but up. As low as you may have felt during a period of something in your life not going the way you planned, somewhere therein laid an opportunity to grow, to start over or to renew. Although the situation hardly looks that way at the time, our experiences with failure are the channel through which we become better and stronger. Instead of looking at your failure as something dying, think of it as something that is emerging.

Gather some silk or real flowers, one to represent each of the major failures you have encountered in life. Arrange them in a vase and look at them as you think about your disappointments and search to find beauty in the outcome of your negative experiences. If you prefer, you can arrange a bowl of fruit or something else that is attractive to you, like party favor diamond rings or trophies.

It's the Situation That Failed, Not Me!

Fill in the blank spaces below with a few words that describe your failures. Then speak them aloud as many times as needed until you feel better about your failed efforts:

It's the _____ that failed, not me!
It's the _____ that failed, not me!
It's the _____ that failed, not me!
It's the _____ that failed, not me!
I am not a failure because my _____.
I am stronger, wiser and better because I made it through all of those tough experiences. I AM a survivor!

Find Your Survivor Mentor

You don't have to know the person, and you may find him or her in your own home. Research stories about people who have survived circumstances similar to what you have been through or something you are afraid you will go through if you follow your destiny. You may find an inspiring story in a book or online. Keep the story conveniently near to read it and remember that survivors are real and they don't just survive. They thrive!

Celebrate Yourself!

While you are traveling the route of Destiny, it may be easy to convince yourself that you can celebrate your accomplishments only after you get to where you want to be. Celebrate now! Buy a congratulatory or a blank card and write a note to yourself, giving yourself praise for how far you've come thus far. Brag on yourself and don't spare the compliments!

Write the card to yourself as you would for someone else who has reached some of the milestones you have. If you've graduated from college with honors or even if you got your degree by the skin of your teeth, affirm the fact that you made it out. Celebrate accomplishments like marriage, job, children, home purchase, weight loss, learning a foreign language, and so forth.

Keep the card and read it occasionally to remind yourself that you deserve to be celebrated and that you are moving forward, even if it's only in small increments.

Break the Shackles of Fear

Living in fear is like living in bondage. Look at the image of shackles and think about your fears. How have you been a prisoner to fear and how has the encumbrance of being afraid held you back from moving within the calling of Destiny?

Did you feel like there were places you couldn't go in your career or in your relationship or finances? Did you feel like life had you on "lockdown"?

_____

_____

_____

_____

_____

What Do You Fear Most?

Answer the following question and explain your answer. Are you more afraid of success or failure? Write your feelings below.

_____

_____

_____

_____

_____

_____

_____

_____

_____

CHAPTER 13

◄►

Pursue Knowledge as Adventure

"If money is your hope for independence you will never have it. The only real security that a man will have in this world is a reserve of knowledge, experience, and ability."

Henry Ford

In the 1980s the *National Inquirer* tabloid used to advertise using the slogan "Inquiring minds want to know." An inquiring mind seeks information beyond the present level of knowledge and experience.

It's fair to assume that you are interested in personal growth since you're using this guide, but some people are disinterested in any type of personal growth. They want to believe what they want to believe and don't want to be enlightened. They don't want to expend the energy to learn new things and expose themselves. They don't want to be challenged by new knowledge. We almost have to wonder why they want to keep living. Their world is very small and maintains itself fueled by insular ignorance.

Admitting ignorance to something brings a certain level of vulnerability. What if someone ridicules you for not knowing? Maybe others will judge you or make assumptions about you. What if they choose not to hire you, or not to associate with you because of what you don't know?

Knowledge carries with it great responsibility and it's somewhat understandable why some people may prefer to stay ignorant. The burden of knowing will cause a man to disregard the signs that his wife is having an affair. If he allows himself to step out of his cloud of ignorance, he will have to deal with issues like whether his wife will leave the marriage, how he has failed as a husband, fighting the images in his mind of his wife being with another man, acknowledging his inadequacies as a husband and/or father. Once the husband admits to himself that he knows, he has to deal with the situation. People sometimes have powerful incentives to maintain ignorance.

Three Powerful Words: "I Don't Know"

Imagine a scenario in which you don't know something that others deem important information. Could you be honest about what you don't know? When you think of the following people, consider whether or not you can be vulnerable and confess your lack of knowledge. How would you explain to them that you don't know something?

- ☐ The company owner where you work
- ☐ An important major client
- ☐ Your spouse
- ☐ Your child
- ☐ Your rival from high school
- ☐ Your student or mentee

Courage to Learn

An extension of the purposefully ignorant is found in the people who remain so because they lack the courage to put themselves in the vulnerable position of admitting their lack of knowledge and then being taught. You need courage to acknowledge what you do not know. It takes audacity to inquire into a world that offers greater knowledge. Strive for an inquiring mind that is perpetually turned toward the far-reaching arms of knowledge.

How have you grown as a result of increased knowledge? What were two major growth opportunities for you? What about those experiences caused you to experience considerable growth?

Think about when you recognized what happened as a growth opportunity. More than likely, what you went through didn't feel like it would be beneficial at the time.

Think about the two experiences you write down and remember them when you endure another difficult situation so you may begin to see it as another means to grow better, stronger, wiser, etc.

Experience 1

_____

_____

_____

_____

_____

_____

Experience 2

_____

_____

_____

_____

_____

_____

_____

Failure Benefits

Think about this sentence: "Redeeming value is in our failures." Think about what the words mean and whether you have found them to be true in your life. In what capacity has failure been redemptive in your life?

_____

_____

_____

_____

_____

_____

Is Failure Really the Worst Thing?

Failure is what we envision as the worst thing that could ever happen to us. Try to think about "failure" in a different way. Think of someone you know who was believed to have failed, but came out on top. What sometimes looks like failure to us is the pivotal action to turn our lives in the true direction toward Destiny.

Create an acronym made from F-A-I-L-U-R-E that will help you rethink what it means to have a life experience where things don't happen as you'd hoped or planned. Each letter in the acronym can be connected to a word, a phrase or a sentence.

F _____

A _____

I _____

L _____

U _____

R _____

E _____

Are You Afraid of Success?

You may be so busy pursuing success that you never have taken the time to consider how utterly frightening it can be to arrive at the place of your most desired dreams. What if you hit the pinnacle of your destiny today? How frightened are you to be around experts in the field? To have reporters camped outside your door? To manage someone else's billion dollar account?

Think about whether you are prepared to operate in your place of Destiny. Then consider what kinds of things you might do to prevent your Destiny experience from becoming anticlimactic.

_____

_____

_____

_____

_____

_____

Why Are Feelings So Scary?

They can't hurt you. They can't kill you. Yet feelings can scare you to the point that you wish you were dead. What you feel can cause you to make irrational moves and have big regrets afterward. What can you do to keep feelings in proper perspective on your Destiny walk so they don't rule you? Instead you tough out the feelings and choose to make sound decisions despite how you feel.

_____

_____

_____

_____

_____

_____

Take a Destiny Step

Think about whether you may be sabotaging your own progress or success and list ways you might be doing so.

_____

_____

_____

_____

_____

_____

_____

_____

_____

_____

CHAPTER 14

✦

Put Your Energy in the Right Places

"You cannot live to please everyone else. You have to edify, educate and fulfill your own dreams and destiny, and hope that whatever your art is that you're putting out there, if it's received, great, I respect you for receiving it. If it's not received, great, I respect you for not."

Octavia Spencer

Passion is a fascinating emotion. This powerful driving force can appear, seemingly out of no place. A quiet, unassuming woman can do a 180-degree turnaround and demonstrate great passion for fighting injustice against children. Conversely, people who appear to have great passion for life may suddenly shut down when faced with a challenge requiring strength and bravado.

Passion is such a powerful sensation that we are wise to use care where to direct its use. A powerful urge can drive us to initiate an enduring movement, like Millard Fuller, founder of Habitat for Humanity, or Clara Hale, also known as Mother Hale. For more than twenty years, Hale cared for babies born to drug-addicted mothers from her home in Harlem, New York. We might be inspired to become champions for justice, like Barry Scheck and Peter Neufeld, who founded The Innocence Project, a non-profit legal organization that is committed to exonerating wrongly convicted men and women through the use of DNA testing.

The most important fact about passion is that you follow what you are authentically driven to do. You can't sustain passion for something simply because it impresses other people. You can't really maintain a strong desire to do what someone else is called to do. A woman may watch her friend marry a successful man and raise three children as a stay-at-mother. She many think, "I want that, too." But if her true passion is to pursue an interest that requires her to delay having a husband and babies, she may be disappointed in both marriage and motherhood that she pursued too soon.

Whose Calling Is It Anyway?

You may have found yourself wishing for someone else's dream at one time or another, perhaps because theirs seemed easier, better, more exciting or more interesting. Why? Think about that person's life. What made their life more appealing than your own? Did they have more things? Better relationships? A better career? Write down some specific features or attributes.

_____ _____ _____

_____ _____ _____

_____ _____ _____

_____ _____ _____

Now, draw a line through the things you don't necessarily want in your life. For example, the person may have a job that requires them to work at least eighty hours each week. That may not appeal to you because you enjoy spending time each week with family and friends. Or maybe the travel schedule of someone you admire makes his position unappealing.

Put a circle around the things you could have, but do not. Write down why you don't have those things and what it would take to get them.

_____ _____

_____ _____

_____ _____

Now, look at the attributes of the other person's life again. Do you really want that life? You probably know that no one's existence is as wonderful at it seems. Everyone has problems.

Truth vs. Reality

Think about the factors in your life that might cause someone to be envious or jealous. Then consider the truth of your situation as well as the reality of your circumstances. For instance, the truth may be that you drive a beautiful luxury car, but the *reality* is sometimes making the monthly payment causes you to make some major financial sacrifices.

What would it take to attain the life you truly desire. What characteristics comprise an authentic life for you? The *truth* is that you may be envied for the beautiful new baby you have, but the *reality* is that you don't get much sleep and are often cranky because the baby frequently keeps you awake at night.

My truth	*My reality*

Life holds both great times and challenges for everyone. As you think about your own, remember that other people have a truth and a reality to their lives as well. Remember that fact whenever you experience feelings of jealousy or envy about the way someone else seems to be living. Determine to use that energy doing something more worthwhile for your own life and your own dream.

Accountability Sheet

What are the gifts God holds you accountable to use? At the end of your life, will you be pleased? If you haven't given life all you have to offer, you may grow older facing a myriad of regrets. For instance, you may have a gift for quick wit, but if you've only used it to sarcastically point out the faults of others, you're wasting it. How about the way you have nurtured your children? What about the way you've used your financial resources? We all make mistakes, and we find a way to keep going and move forward so we can do better.

List some of your most prominent gifts and abilities. If you don't know what they are ask a friend or family member to help you identify the things you do best. Then place a star next to the talents you are using to the best of your ability. Place a check mark by those areas where you can do more, and then determine how you can live fulfilling all that God has gifted you to accomplish.

_____ _____ _____

_____ _____ _____

_____ _____ _____

_____ _____ _____

It's Bigger Than You

To ensure that your vision for your destiny is not self-serving, think about whether your plans and goals are bigger than you. If they're not, think about how the dreams you desire can be used to serve humanity in a greater way.

Write your goals in one of the circles below. Place each in the appropriate circle, depending on whether you think it will serve you only or will have a greater impact on humanity.

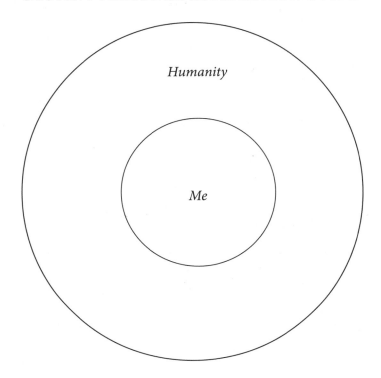

Put on the Proper Head Gear

Destiny is a journey that has ups and downs. During the up times, you may be prone to minimize your accomplishments. During the down times, putting yourself down for not having done more can be tempting. All those conversations happen between your ears, so it's important to tell yourself messages that uplift and encourage you to keep going.

Choose an inspiring message that can help you direct your self-talk when you are challenged by circumstances, or when something good happens and you can find the words to congratulate yourself.

Type them on a strip of paper and keep it in your wallet or mobile phone case. Enlarge the type and print it on a sheet of paper to hang on your wall. Use it as a screen saver or place it somewhere else in a prominent location.

Consider some of the following examples:

"Don't judge each day by the harvest you reap but by the seeds that you plant."

Robert Louis Stevenson

"Only those who will risk going too far can possibly find out how far one can go."

T. S. Eliot

"He who is not courageous enough to take risks will accomplish nothing in life."
Muhammad Ali

"The more you praise and celebrate your life, the more there is in life to celebrate."

Oprah Winfrey

"Your time is limited, so don't waste it living someone else's life. Don't be trapped by dogma—which is living with the results of other people's thinking. Don't let the noise of others' opinions drown out your own inner voice. And most important, have the courage to follow your heart and intuition."
Steve Jobs

"It is in your moments of decision that your destiny is shaped."
Tony Robbins

"When I stand before God at the end of my life, I would hope that I would not have a single bit of talent left, and could say, 'I used everything you gave me.'"
Erma Bombeck

What Do You Say to Yourself?

Carry a sheet of paper or a pocket-sized small notebook with you for one full day. Every time you talk to yourself about you, write down what you told yourself.

How many of your self-talk messages were encouraging? How many are unconstructive? Which statements were merited (good or bad) and which were said out of habit? What's your positive-negative talk ratio? If you spend more time giving yourself critical messages than positive ones, it's time to be more intentional about monitoring the things you say to yourself.

After you monitor your self-talk, repeat the exercise by paying attention to the way others talk to you. You may want to do this over a period of several days. Who are the people who affirm you? Who are the people that are always putting you down, even in a joking way?

After several days give some consideration to how you may need to restructure some friendships or relationships so that you do not continue to expose yourself to constant negative messaging from the people with whom you spend the most time.

Kicking Yourself Out of the Comfort Zone

Let's face it. We like comfort. None of us relishes the thought of struggle and we usually do everything we can to avoid any form of distress. We want to know that all is well at home, at work or school, with our physical and financial well-being and with our relationships. In an ideal world, we would live in a sustained comfort zone that maintained an even level of stability, much like a thermostat regulates the temperature in our home.

We become like thermometers over our lives. At any sign of trouble we step in and attempt to regulate the situation to sustain our comfort. But sometimes God's plan does not include maintaining the status quo. Sometimes, God's plan allows our circumstances to simply get hotter and hotter until we are uncomfortable enough to make a move.

Sometimes, striving to maintain the current level in our lives is not enough. We must go higher. Think of it like this: You may be afraid of what will happen when you let go because you don't know what discomfort you may find there. But if you're already uncomfortable trying to sustain, why not take the risk of moving away from the familiar to have a greater life?

Take a look at all of your activities and relationships. Are you sitting in a comfort zone in some area? Are you dating a man who is not marriage material just because he's there? Is your job unfulfilling, but safe? Did you stop pursuing higher education simply because it got too hard? Have you adopted a healthier diet and lost a few pounds but stopped short of working out to improve your physical condition?

After you identify those areas, think of at least one realistic step that will help you to move away from the false security of a comfort zone and align with the path of your destiny. If you need additional education or training, a realistic first step is to determine which schools offer the training that you need. If you already know that, then determine which school you can afford to attend and how you can obtain tuition assistance. If you already know that, then complete the application. The point is to take a step so that the entire process doesn't seem so frightening and overwhelming.

Comfort Zone	*Initial Step*
_____	_____
_____	_____
_____	_____
_____	_____
_____	_____

What Do You Bring to the Zone?

What do you bring to the creative zone? Think about your abilities that make you uniquely you. In the following Creative Zone, write down the things you have to offer that no one else can—inventiveness, insight, creativity, humor, intellect, reason, special skills. Like a specialty recipe, the mix of ingredients you bring makes you a unique creation.

What's the creative recipe that makes you distinctly you? As you add the ingredients, determine how many parts. Perhaps you bring a lot of intellect with a bit of humor, or a lot of humor with a bit of insight and a lot of expertise in a particular area. You may be three parts intellect and one part humor, or four parts wisdom with four parts expertise. Look at your recipe to remember that you are a custom-made creation of God, designed for a unique purpose. Think of ten parts of you that would prove beneficial in any situation.

My Recipe

_____ _____

_____ _____

_____ _____

_____ _____

_____ _____

_____ _____

_____ _____

_____ _____

_____ _____

_____ _____

Move into the Creative Zone

The Creative Zone is like a neighborhood where some live, others can't seem to find the street, and still others don't even know that it exists. Think about people you know who live in the creative zone and decide who you want to live in that neighborhood with. Write your own name, along with the names of people who may be helpful to align with as you travel the Destiny road.

Creative Zone

Take a Destiny Step

Commit to look in the mirror every day for at least one week and speak words of empowerment and courage. Remind yourself that you are uniquely created by God and you have much to offer in God's service through the fulfillment of your destiny.

You may discover that speaking encouragement to yourself daily is a great way to start or complete your day. Write a sample statement of empowerment below.

_____

_____

_____

_____

CHAPTER 15

Destiny Is Calling You

"Man is supposed to be the maker of his destiny. It is only partly true. He can make his destiny, only in so far as he is allowed by the Great Power."

Mahatma Gandhi

Just Listen

There are all types of voices calling out to you at any given point during the day. You will have many different voices of your own speaking to you. They're there. Admit it, introduce yourself to each of them, and even have fun talking back to them and listening.

Create a name for each of the voices you hear. Once you identify them, you can learn to have greater control over the influence they have over you. Name your encouraging voice, your critical voice, the childish brat voice, the complainer voice, the tough love voice, your suck-it-up voice, the unconditional love voice, the comedian voice, and any others that speak to you. Recognize that each has a place in your life. Each voice deserves to be heard. The problem arises when you allow a single voice to dominate what you can listen to.

If you only allow the childish brat to speak, then you will spend your life blaming others for your circumstances and being angry when things don't go your way. If no one but the comedian talks, then everything becomes one big joke, even when the situation isn't funny.

By identifying the voices in your head, you can control when and how they speak to you. When they speak, you can allow them to keep talking or tell them to be quiet. It may sound crazy, but since the voices are already there, you might as well name them and get acquainted with them so you can be in control of the internal conversations of your mind.

Voice	*Name*
_____	_____
_____	_____
_____	_____
_____	_____
_____	_____

Hearing Outside Voices

Who are the outside voices that you are most likely to listen to? Spouse? Parent? Best friend? Children? Grandparent? Boss?

Write down the names of people you really listen to, and then write down a couple of reasons why you listen to them. Hopefully, your rationale will be more substantial than the relationship you have with them. For example, you may listen to your father about law school because he also has been to law school, but you wouldn't listen to your brother, who barely completed high school.

Person	*Rationale for Listening*
_____	_____
_____	_____

_____   _____

_____   _____

_____   _____

_____   _____

_____   _____

Look at the list carefully. Understand why you listen to them. If you are listening to someone, but there's no sound rationale why you do, perhaps it's time to rethink what advice you will take in the future and from whom.

Give Yourself Permission Not to Tell

Your journey to Destiny can seem very precarious at times. You will have occasions when you wonder if you're making a mistake. During those periods of extreme vulnerability, you can't afford to leave yourself open to haters. The best defense against haters in the developmental stage is not telling them the dreams that are closest to your heart.

It's okay not to tell your dreams to just anybody. It's healthy to identify the safe people in your life and share your successes with them. You will have enough haters once you begin to rise, so don't give them a head start!

Identify your safe people with whom to share your vision. Look around for the people who are already content with their own accomplishments, or who are trying in earnest to fulfill their own destiny. These are the people who will share in your joy and encourage you to keep going when you feel as though you're breaking.

Those you trust will be the chosen few. Don't worry if you only have a couple of names. You really shouldn't have that many people you trust so intimately. Next to each name, write down why you know this is a "safe place" person in your life.

How has that person demonstrated the ability to extend trust, encouragement, love and support to you for any good thing you choose to do? Write the names of the few people you can go to and confess failure or celebrate victory. You may even know some people you can share parts of your journey with but not others. That's okay, too. You may have a friend who will celebrate you asking your girlfriend to be your wife, but that same person cannot rejoice in you quitting your job to start your own business.

Place an asterisk by the names of people who can be trusted with information about certain areas of your life.

<table>
<tr><td align="center">*Who?*</td><td align="center">*What Area?*</td></tr>
<tr><td>_____</td><td>_____</td></tr>
<tr><td>_____</td><td>_____</td></tr>
<tr><td>_____</td><td>_____</td></tr>
<tr><td>_____</td><td>_____</td></tr>
<tr><td>_____</td><td>_____</td></tr>
<tr><td>_____</td><td>_____</td></tr>
<tr><td>_____</td><td>_____</td></tr>
</table>

Handle the Haters

How do you deal with the negative commentary of a hater? Sometimes we're so caught off guard by the vitriol that we're speechless. When you are slammed by such negativity, sometimes the best response is no response. But there are other ways to respond; such has holding haters accountable for their words. For example:

- ☐ What do you mean by that?
- ☐ I want to be sure I understand. You're saying I'm…
- ☐ Why does it matter to you what I'm doing?

You can also hold haters accountable by not buying into their pessimism. But it's also important to remember these truths:

- ☐ Their hate isn't about who you are, it's about who they're not.
- ☐ Their hate is more about them than about you.
- ☐ Most haters are insecure about who they are and what they have not accomplished.
- ☐ You may be overlooking the well-wishes of ninety-eight people while you're focusing on the negativity of two.
- ☐ What someone else thinks of you is none of your business.

Why Bother to Care?

Think about the people you know who fit into these categories. Then ask yourself, "Why would I care what he/she thinks?" Read the following message of affirmation to conduct a mental cleansing from the negativity.

I affirm you _____, and hope you will have positive, uplifting thoughts about yourself so you can begin to have positive thoughts about others.

I cannot be brought down by the negative opinions of haters. I will not fuel their negative energy by retaliating with feelings of jealousy, envy or criticism.

I cannot control what another person thinks about my actions. What _____ thinks of me is none of my business.

Everybody Has Them

Have you ever listened to someone speak authoritatively on a topic and find out later that person was terribly wrong? We must remember that when it comes to opinions. It's just that. Every person has them, and they can be as right or wrong as anyone else's.

Who do you know that has given an opinion about something that was later proven wrong? Sometimes even so-called experts are proven terribly wrong. Recall the experience. The person may never have discovered that he or she was wrong. That's not important anyway. What is important is that you remember that opinions are as varied as the people who offer them. Remind yourself of this truth frequently, so that you do not fall prey to the trap of human opinion.

Find a quote online about opinions and write it here to help you remember their subjective nature.

_____

_____

_____

_____

This may be a good time for some reflection to think about finding your balance between heeding the wise counsel of someone you respect versus the opinion of someone who simply wants to share a personal point of view.

The Most Dangerous People You Know

You may be like most of us, who at one time or another associated with people who have no dreams, no goals, and nothing to lose. These are the very people who will try and convince you to do something illegal or take a shortcut to Destiny because working for it will take too much time.

Think about a couple of people you know who lost a great deal because of their association with people who had no dreams, no hopes, and nothing to lose. Name them here. Who contributed to their demise? Family members? Childhood friends? Significant other?

_____

_____

_____

_____

_____

As you map out the details of the person's demise, think about your own life and how you can guard against close associations with people who can take you down because your demise won't cost them anything.

Shhhh! Destiny Is Speaking

How often do you get still enough to listen? Where can you do it? After everyone else in the house is asleep, you're exhausted. After a long day at work you're tired and just want to unwind with a little television. Instead of television, give yourself the gift of soothing music—not the kind that makes you want to get up and dance, nor the genre that causes you to reminisce about past loves.

Listen to music that will calm and quiet you. Walk or drive to a nearby park. If you're driving, find a spot and turn off the engine with the windows down. Hear the sounds of nature. Listen to the un-noise of silence. Don't be upset if your mind wanders. You've got lots on your mind. But as your schedule downtime for your life, you will get better at it.

Quiet Time Schedule

Schedule your quiet times until you acquire the art of listening. As you learn to listen for the voice of Destiny, you will hear it, even when there is other noise around you.

Where can you schedule time to get quiet?

Home (time/place) _____

Work (time/place) _____

Auto (time/place) _____

Weekend home (time/place) _____

Evenings home (time/place) _____

As you schedule your quiet time, respect the appointment that you've made with yourself. Treat it as sacred as you would an appointment made with another person. Keep you appointment to train your ears to hear the sound of Destiny.

Take a Destiny Step

Determine the people, actions and behaviors that have nothing to do with your destiny. What voices do you need to block from your ears?

_____

_____

_____

_____

_____

CHAPTER 16

✦

Expose and Expand

"If you want to know the taste of a pear, you must change the pear by eating it yourself. If you want to know the theory and methods of revolution, you must take part in revolution. All genuine knowledge originates in direct experience."

Mao Zedong

As you've worked through the book and this companion guide, you are probably pumped up about working your way to, and actually reaching the place in life where you are destined to be. If you are faithful to the path Destiny calls you to, you will see glimpses along the way. As excited as you may be about seeing your future unfold, it can be a bit frightening and daunting as well.

How would you respond if you were suddenly in a room filled with the people who have reached the pinnacle of your field of Destiny? That would be exciting, but wouldn't it be a bit intimidating, too? That's why exposure along the way is so important. It prevents you from zipping to the top too soon and then running away because you feel you don't belong.

Getting exposure can mean leaving the familiar behind and being open to where you've never been. If you were raised in the projects, you might have associated with people who eschewed anyone who "talked white" and made good grades. Now, as you're applying for law schools and associating with people who have the power to offer you internships or fellowships, you may begin to feel like you're betraying your heritage in order to get ahead. But let's be real. You won't make inroads into your dream vocation if you can't leave certain elements of your past behind. Or maybe you want to get into the music business, particularly hip-hop, but you grew up in a white, upper-middle-class neighborhood where everyone looked like you and had the same experiences as you. In order to be successful, you'll need exposure, because you won't make it by thinking that what you see on music videos and reality shows is all there is to it. You'll need exposure to a culture that will allow you to understand and relate. You will have to put aside socioeconomic prejudices so you aren't booted out of the business before you get in the door good.

What Destiny Looks Like

If you were at your Destiny spot right now, who from your past or current circle will have been left behind and why? If what you need to leave behind is not a person, write it down also, along with the understanding of why you need to step away from it.

Who/What?	*Why?*
_____	_____
_____	_____
_____	_____
_____	_____
_____	_____

Don't Get It Twisted

When the Destiny journey gets tough, we have a tendency to glamorize the past. You need a realistic assessment, however, so you can avoid the temptation to want to run back there. Write down every major situation you've left behind, followed by an honest description of what it was like then and why it wouldn't be a good idea to go back.

Complete this exercise at a time when you are feeling optimistic about your future. For example, you may have a great, but high-pressure job right now because of your learning curb. You know this is where you want to be, but sometimes it's so stressful you reminisce about the carefree days of your previous job. The expectations there were low, so you had lots of time to goof off with co-workers. But don't forget, the pay and the opportunities there were equally as low. The boyfriend you walked away from because he had no ambition still has no ambition, and you couldn't have changed him.

Write about past relationships, past jobs or employment opportunities, previous living conditions, former activities and engagements. Paint a realistic picture that will always remind you of why you are no longer at that place, nor do you want to be.

Relationships

_____

_____

_____

_____

_____

_____

_____

_____

_____

_____

_____

_____

_____

_____

_____

_____

_____

Employment or Job Opportunities

_____

_____

_____

_____

_____

_____

_____

_____

_____

_____

_____

_____

_____

_____

_____

_____

_____

Housing/Neighborhood

_____

_____

Activities/Habits

_____

_____

_____

_____

_____

_____

_____

_____

Other Situations Left Behind

_____

_____

_____

_____

_____

_____

_____

_____

_____

_____

_____

_____

_____

Help Exposure Help You

There are times when opportunities serendipitously appear, but most of the time they come because we have done the work to position ourselves for the next big break.

Exposure doesn't come knocking at your door; it may not even come because you're sitting at your desk working hard every day. We have to actively pursue the opportunities we want.

Write down the opportunities you would like to have. Then write down the steps you can take to help create those situations (volunteer, part-time job, community group, etc).

Opportunity

_____

_____

Personal Steps to Create

_____

_____

Opportunity

_____

_____

Personal Steps to Create

_____

_____

Opportunity

_____

_____

Personal Steps to Create

_____

_____

Can Exposure Help?

How can exposure help you most? Do you need to erase some prejudices? Are you small-minded or judgmental about certain people? Have you formed certain hard-core opinions about people who are wealthy or poor, educated or uneducated, or of a certain racial heritage? Take a self-assessment to determine how exposure can help you be more prepared for your destiny.

_____

_____

_____

_____

_____

_____

_____

_____

_____

_____

_____

What Exposure Can Do

Read the following statements made in the book about exposure and its importance to Destiny. How many of these statements have already proven true in your life? Place a check mark next to the experiences you have already had with exposure.

- ☐ Exposure is empowering because it can mold, shape, and change you.
- ☐ Exposure broadens your thinking.
- ☐ Exposure teaches you that there is more than one way of doing things.
- ☐ Exposure is all about conscious choices.
- ☐ Part of the challenge to gaining more exposure is pushing past the feelings of discomfort as you acclimate to your new environment.

☐ When the discomfort of your new environment makes you fearful, ride the wave of feelings long enough to give it a good test-drive.

☐ Exposure also helps you know what you don't want.

☐ Choosing exposure will require you to look at things differently and pay attention to life again.

Open Doors to Exposure

Have you closed some doors Destiny was trying to open for you? We do that by passing on to others opportunities that are meant for us. We recommend others for a job we want but feel someone else may be more qualified. We may not feel we're ready for the type of recognition that comes with exposure.

Think about whether you have pushed Destiny opportunities aside. Sometimes you may have recognized them as such at the time. Write them down so that you will be more aware of the kinds of ways opportunities for exposure can manifest.

_____

_____

_____

_____

_____

_____

_____

_____

_____

_____

Exposure doesn't necessarily mean world travel or working at a Fortune 100 company. You can broaden your mind-set through a variety of activities. Look at the list below and determine which may be realistic options for you.

- ☐ Reading
- ☐ Cultural Events
- ☐ College-level elective course
- ☐ Athletic activities/exercise
- ☐ Volunteer at a help agency
- ☐ Usher at a local concern venue
- ☐ Philanthropic activities
- ☐ Tutoring children or adults
- ☐ Visiting local library
- ☐ Joining committees for major community events

Oak or Willow?

Oak trees are known and appreciated for being solid, tall, strong and unmovable. We like the notion of strength, that we are unmoved by our circumstances. And to a certain extent, that's true. We need to remain strong so that our situations don't define us. When we are strong like the mighty oak, we will not compromise our integrity, our values or our beliefs because our circumstances change, either for better or for worse.

As good as it is to be an oak, when it comes to traveling Destiny's road, we do well to adopt the habits of the willow. These trees also grow tall, but they have the ability to move with changing winds so that they do not snap and break against the force of changing winds.

You may have situations born into your life, or they may come as a result of something dying. Either way things happen for us, we are best postured for Destiny when we are willing to move with the flow of life and accept the circumstances that are born into our lives, as well as the things that are taken away, thus making room for something else.

The winds of life can change quickly. If you have determined to be an oak all of your life, you will encounter difficulty when unexpected conditions push against your circumstances. No one should bend with every changing wind, but we must be adaptable, because in the movements we find opportunities to move closer to Destiny.

How rigid are you? How do you react to change? Write your responses below.

Changes at home

_____

_____

_____

_____

Physical changes

_____

_____

_____

_____

Changes at work

_____

_____

_____

_____

_____

Changes in relationships

_____

_____

_____

_____

_____

Changes at community

_____

_____

_____

_____

_____

If you realize that you do not adapt well to change, try to find out why. Sometimes our upbringing conditions us to accept or reject change. Even factors like birth order can impact our ability to be flexible in life situations. Give some thought to the life experiences that cause you to be the way you are, then determine where changes may be needed to help you not close yourself off from Destiny opportunities.

_____

_____

_____

_____

_____

Lost Grace

You may have lost your grace for tolerating, or even enjoying certain activities or people or circumstances. What are they? Figure out why you've lost your grace and whether the loss is an indication that it's time to move on and inch closer to Destiny.

_____

_____

_____

_____

_____

_____

_____

_____

_____

_____

_____

_____

_____

_____

_____

Take a Destiny Step

Determine one step you can take right now to increase your level of exposure in an area of your life where you are lacking. Volunteer, take a class, read a book, or meet new acquaintances. Prayerfully decide what that step will be and commit to it today.

_____

_____

_____

_____

CHAPTER 17

✥

Who Are You to Strive for Destiny?

"Our deepest fear is not that we are inadequate. Our deepest fear is that we are powerful beyond measure. It is our light, not our darkness that most frightens us. We ask ourselves, Who am I to be brilliant, gorgeous, talented, fabulous? Actually, who are you not to be? You are a child of God. Your playing small does not serve the world. There is nothing enlightened about shrinking so that other people won't feel insecure around you. We are all meant to shine, as children do. We were born to make manifest the glory of God that is within us. It's not just in some of us; it's in everyone. And as we let our own light shine, we unconsciously give other people permission to do the same. As we are liberated from our own fear, our presence automatically liberates others."

From A Return to Love, *by Marianne Williamson*

Why You?

Answer this question: Who am I to have a destiny?

_____

_____

What's Most Important?

What is the most important aspect of Destiny to you? Are you more concerned about economic, social, commercial, or professional success? Why do you most want to achieve your destiny?

_____

_____

_____

_____

_____

_____

_____

_____

Do Others Factor into Your Destiny?

Do you have family or friends who try to persuade you to follow a life path that does not interest you? What do they want for you versus what you want for yourself?

Other people's expectations   *My priority*

_____   _____

_____   _____

_____   _____

_____   _____

_____   _____

_____   _____

Insert your name here

"I, _____, have a unique purpose and a destiny that is distinct from any other person who has ever lived."

Affirm this statement each day, several times a day as you grow to accept that God has assigned a unique destiny for you.

Why Be Normal?

Most of us just want to fit in and be "normal." Think about areas of your life where you simply don't fit in with the people you see around you, either for social, economic, physical, educational, racial, cultural or spiritual reasons.

How can you make your difference an advantage? How can you look differently at your difference and transform your dissimilarity into a Destiny step?

Social

_____

_____

_____

_____

_____

_____

Economic

_____

_____

_____

_____

Physical

_____

_____

_____

_____

Educational

_____

_____

Racial

_____

_____

_____

_____

_____

_____

Cultural

_____

_____

_____

_____

_____

Spritual

_____

_____

_____

_____

_____

Other

_____

_____

_____

_____

_____

The Courage of Authenticity

Why is being your authentic self the most courageous Destiny step you can take?

_____

_____

_____

_____

_____

_____

_____

_____

_____

_____

_____

_____

_____

_____

_____

Don't Undo What God Has Done

How have you neutralized God's creative design of you at those times when you pretended to be like others just so you could fit in?

_____

_____

_____

Watch Out!

Who are the horror movie characters in your life? More than likely, you've met some vampires, the charming types who lure you in but will suck the lifeblood out of you. Then there are the flesh-eating zombies who are unthinking, flesh eaters. They destroy because that's all they know how to do.

They're in the world and you can't avoid them, but what you can do is figure out how to not let them bring you down. First, though, you have to figure out who they are in your life.

How can the steps given in the book on navigating the drama and excitement of striving for Destiny be applied to your life right now?

1. Don't feed on drama.

_____

_____

_____

_____

_____

_____

_____

2. Stay with the strategy.

_____

_____

_____

_____

_____

_____

_____

3. Don't court the undead drama.

_____

_____

_____

_____

_____

_____

_____

4. Distinguish vampires from zombies.

Vampires   *Zombies*

_____   _____

_____   _____

_____   _____

_____   _____

_____   _____

_____   _____

5. Keep it moving.

_____

_____

_____

_____

_____

_____

_____

_____

The Cost of Destiny

Destiny decisions have a price. That price is different for every person. What does the price of Destiny look like in your life? Does it mean lost relationships? Leaving the old neighborhood behind? Acquiring more education? Changing vocations? Making strategic health moves? Shrewd financial planning?

Fear Can Paralyze You

Fear can be a powerful motivator or deterrent. We can become irrational if we are blinded by terror. Take an honest assessment of your life and think about the things you are afraid of and whether that fear is hindering you from taking another step toward Destiny.

How has fear hindered you from any aspect of your destiny? Did it stop you from taking a job or from marrying someone your family disapproved of? Did you tear up the college application? Were you afraid to ask for a date? Ask for a job? Move out of the old neighborhood?

_____

_____

_____

_____

_____

_____

_____

_____

_____

_____

_____

_____

_____

What Are You Scared Of?

What are your fears? How can you overcome them? Are you willing to take the steps necessary to move beyond fear? The action you take may include confronting what you fear, professional counseling, or healing old wounds.

_____

_____

_____

_____

_____

_____

_____

_____

_____

_____

_____

_____

_____

_____

Who's Waiting on Whom?

Find a quiet space and meditate on the following question: "Am I waiting on God, or is God waiting on me?" The place you find may be a park, a walk through the neighborhood, or even a comfortable rocking chair on your front porch. Use the space below to make notes of the thoughts that arose during your time of reflection.

_____

_____

_____

_____

_____

_____

What's the Worst That Could Happen?

When fear paralyzes us, it often does so because we fear the worst. But really, what is the worst thing that could happen if things don't go the way you planned? Allow yourself time to indulge your fearful thoughts. What if the worst thing happened? Play out that scenario, and then determine what you could do to come out of the failed circumstance.

Think about whether there is any situation that you could never rebound from. Hopefully, after this exercise, you will realize that even if your worst fears come true, you can overcome them.

_____

_____

_____

_____

_____

_____

_____

_____

_____

_____

_____

Destiny Is Not Done with You

There's always someplace else for you to rise higher. You can be wealthy, but struggling in your relationships. You may be socially well-connected, but need to be more technologically savvy. Where are the places you have left to go? And, even if you believe you've reached the pinnacle in one area of you life, Destiny may have more places for you to go.

Where do you hope Destiny will still take you?

Professionally

_____

_____

_____

_____

_____

_____

Relationally

_____

_____

_____

_____

_____

_____

_____

_____

Emotionally

_____

_____

_____

_____

_____

_____

_____

Physically

_____

_____

_____

_____

_____

_____

_____

_____

Financially

_____

_____

_____

_____

_____

_____

Spiritually

_____

_____

_____

_____

_____

_____

_____

_____

Take a Destiny Step

Hold to the firm conviction that you have what it takes to strive for the desires of your heart and to fulfill the purpose for which God created you.

Write a promise to yourself that you will hold on to your destiny and not let go.

_____

_____

_____

_____

_____